The Training Ground

William S. McMorrine

Printed in the United States of America

First Printing August 2015

ISBN 978-1-943842-14-8 Paperback

Published by:

Book Services
www.BookServices.us

Contents

Foreword

Lux Esto[1]

This planet Earth is a training ground for your soul, a boot camp to prepare you for a realm of being beyond anything your earthly mind can imagine, a place that some call Heaven. Within the pages of this book you will find the secrets of getting into Heaven. Keeping some secrets is okay, but this is one secret that should not be kept. Why? Because we should strive to get more back from the Devil than the rascal would like us to; we should pull the rug out from under his feet as often as we are able.

The ideas presented herein are based on my own life experience, combined with decades of study, reading, and discussion. In my lengthy dissertations on the Biblical interpretations of these ideas, I do not know that others are in error. However my thinking has led me along a wee bit different path than the one most have taken, and I feel called to guide others along my wildwood path.

I would like to introduce you to a new pastime, The Pursuit of Truth Profound. It will be difficult and challenging, and you may grow weary from the effort, but I believe the reward is the best there is: transformation and redemption. The farther I journey along this path, the more joy I find. So let's call it The Path of Mirth.

---

1   Latin: Let there be light.

The story I tell is revealed in bits and pieces, bytes and pixels. The words used are from the ancients, whose knowledge stretches back over thousands of years.

Even here in North America, thinking people have been passing down their wisdom for millennia. We know they have been here for a very, very long time because twelve to fourteen thousand years ago, these ancient peoples started leaving coprolites in the caves of Eastern Oregon. (My daughter, a Rosicrucian docent, loves to give these gems as gifts.)

This path of mirth I follow scuttles present religious Sunday school rhetoric. For example, the very first story in the Bible, the Garden of Eden narrative, is traditionally taught with the wrong character in the main role. Fast forward to the New Testament and the visit of the wise men. These characters always seem to show up in Christmas displays where they are seen hanging out in the manger in Bethlehem. In reality, they did not visit Jesus until he was two years old and living in Bethlehem.

> The **Paisley Caves** complex is a system of eight caves in an arid, desolate region of south-central Oregon, United States. One of the caves may contain archaeological evidence of the oldest definitively-dated human presence in North America. The site was first studied by archeologists in the 1930s.
>
> Scientific excavations and analysis since 2002 have uncovered substantial new discoveries. These include materials with the oldest DNA evidence of human habitation in North America. The DNA, radiocarbon dated to 14,300 years ago, was found in fossilized human coprolites (feces) uncovered in the Paisley Five Mile Point Caves in south-central Oregon. The caves were added to the National Register of Historic Places in 2014.
>
> Wikipedia

It is not my job to convert you or anyone else to my way of life. That is up to you. If I am wrong, show me the way. What you want to believe is your prerogative. It has no bearing on my own relationship with the Almighty or my getting into heaven. My position is that there ought to be discussions, not confrontations with a goal of conversions. If you differ in opinion from me, please stand on a Bible passage. Do not give me, "I think." Opinion without backup documentation will not hold water.

On the other hand, in our conversations I keep telling the Holy Ghost that he is being lazy if he is unable to get you to believe what is true and not make stuff up.

God is an ornery ol' Soul. In this book we will delve into the plan He has concocted in an effort to regain His leadership here on earth, a plan which involves your gaining ever more knowledge, insight, and experience. It is a plan to entice His followers into doing His wishes in reclaiming the Planet Earth.

Some would call this plan "The New World Order." Here, I'm using this phrase in a very old sense because it isn't really a new idea. It goes all the way back to the folks who came to New England in the 1600s with a dream of creating a great nation in which there would be neither rich nor poor, a nation in which seeking wisdom and knowledge would have priority over material things. Is that ideal so far-fetched? I don't think so.

What is going on today is a battle between God and His son Lucifer. After being kicked out of Heaven by the archangel Michael, Lucifer is in charge here on earth, and he is *very* capable. And very clever. You may find it surprising, but in my analysis Satan is also a necessary part of the plan.

Lucifer was one of God's favorites, and according to legend, he was most beautiful. So what's the story? Well, here's how I picture the deal between God and Lucifer going down. God has Lucifer come into His office, and after much discussion, they enter into a partnership in education, *your* education.

Lucifer will receive an elevated position here on earth as the King of the Underworld. He loves that title. God will keep two thirds of the host of Heaven (the souls). Satan will have the remaining third of the host of heaven for his worshipers. The members of this host will have opportunities, comforts, and wealth. All they will have to do is sell their souls to Lucifer.

With Lucifer's new red body suit and long tail, forked on the end, comes a new name, Satan. We now have our first corporation on Planet Earth. The name of this mega business is Good & Evil, Inc. No doubt it will be successful, for both the good people *and* the evil people will all be contributing to its coffers. This is not a blast at the churches. Church is a contrivance that God and Satan have allowed man to create. God is a jealous God, not a stingy God.

Satan is doing his job well. He instills in the well-off an ever-increasing and insatiable hunger for more – a hunger to advance from being well-off to being rich, and then from rich to very rich. As soon as one level of comfort and wealth is attained, another appears that is more desirable and more tantalizing just over the horizon.

In order for the upwardly mobile to attain the desired level of wealth, however, it is necessary to control the lesser minions. For example, it is necessary for legislators to be infected with the same highly contagious lust, so that they will make the rules for the benefit of those accumulating more and more earthly treasure. America was founded on the idea of equality, not aristocracy. Sadly, the gap between rich and poor has widened from a crack to a chasm in the twenty-first century.

Jesus tells us that the rich will have as much difficulty achieving admission into Heaven as would a camel passing through the eye of a needle. Not only does the camel have its hump to deal with, but now it is also overloaded with earthly goods. Most legislation is crafted to keep the motley minions in their place. People in power are terrified of losing their power. They use their discretionary funds to entice elected persons to make the rules in their favor. Satan is an expert at psychological manipulation.

What can you yourself do to remedy this problem? How can you one-up Satan? You can study. You can learn. I assure you that it will pay off.

Earth is a training ground where your assignment is increasing your knowledge. In heaven, there are no opportunities to advance one's knowledge. Where would you go to school? Would you wear a school uniform? Would they have report cards? School lunch programs?

Don't worry. Your school is right here. The Almighty has an educational plan for you. It concerns your two souls: your earthly soul and your celestial soul.

The Almighty sends *you*, a celestial soul from heaven, down here to Earth, the Training Ground, to be a warrior in the battle of good and evil. Your celestial soul has been endowed with a terrestrial body for the time that you are here on this planet in full view of God and the Son of Perdition.

You will receive assistance from heaven. God will provide the toolbox. You will learn to open your terrestrial soul and listen to the voice within. The voice within is *you*, the celestial soul in this earthly body. At times this voice is very loud, and at other times it is barely loud enough to discern, just the merest whisper.

But that voice is there, and the job of your celestial soul is to enlist the body, your temple here on earth, to listen to you and the Holy Ghost and live accordingly. The body is going to be a tough guy to convince, especially when God tells the earthling to be fruitful and multiply. The body loves *that* role. Does the soul cherish offspring? Let the Almighty set the example.

There are many methods the Almighty employs to ensure that you will have some difficulty in achieving a passing grade here on earth. Does this seem unfair? No. You can't build a muscle without putting stress on it. Likewise, you can't build spiritual muscle without challenges.

In heaven, as a means of relaxation, the Almighty and His cohorts have developed a beverage, the nectar of the Gods. (This earthly body sure as the dickens is going to like that.) God sends His Son down here, and what happens? Jesus is judged by his fellow Jews as being a winebibber and glutton.

Satan Necessary to Learning. Satan is the source of greater understanding. One must be in Satan's presence to get smarter. The soul is *you*. This earthly body we inhabit for a time is the classroom. The job of the soul is to entice the human mind to rule this body with the rules of heaven and not the rules of earth.

One of the pitfalls the Almighty has inserted into this classroom is the command to be fruitful and multiply, while also ultimately requiring celibacy in order to gain entry into heaven.

On the other hand, when exam time comes, you will not be tempted beyond your strength, and there will always be a way for you to escape. You just have to learn to see the open door.

The Almighty does reveal the truth, but only to those diligent in seeking instruction. It is written that He tested Abraham. What temptations does he place before *you*?

1 Corinthians 10:13: "There hath no temptation taken you but such as is common to man: but God is faithful, who will not suffer you to be tempted above that ye are able; but will with the temptation also make a way to escape, that ye may be able to bear it." A good drill sergeant wants to end up with a good soldier, not a dead soldier. This verse shows that there is redemption."

The story of Abraham and his son Isaac adds considerable interest to the Biblical narrative on temptation. It's not just about temptation; it's about faith and prophetic truth. The Russian writer Dostoevsky said, "A son can kill a father, but a father does not kill his son." Dostoevsky understood that the psychology of such a situation is very complicated. Abraham's story appears again in the book of Hebrews in the New Testament.

Genesis 22 (King James Version)

1. And it came to pass after these things, that God did tempt Abraham, and said unto him, Abraham: and he said, Behold, here I am.

2. And he said, Take now thy son, thine only son Isaac, whom thou lovest, and get thee into the land of Moriah; and offer him there for a burnt offering upon one of the mountains which I will tell thee of.

3. And Abraham rose up early in the morning, and saddled his ass, and took two of his young men with him, and Isaac his son, and clave the wood for the burnt offering, and rose up, and went unto the place of which God had told him.

4. Then on the third day Abraham lifted up his eyes, and saw the place afar off.

5. And Abraham said unto his young men, Abide ye here with the ass; and I and the lad will go yonder and worship, and come again to you.

6. And Abraham took the wood of the burnt offering, and laid it upon Isaac his son; and he took the fire in his hand, and a knife; and they went both of them together.

7. And Isaac spake unto Abraham his father, and said, My father: and he said, Here am I, my son. And he said, Behold the fire and the wood: but where is the lamb for a burnt offering?

8. And Abraham said, My son, God will provide himself a lamb for a burnt offering: so they went both of them together.

9. And they came to the place which God had told him of; and Abraham built an altar there, and laid the wood in order, and bound Isaac his son, and laid him on the altar upon the wood.

10. And Abraham stretched forth his hand, and took the knife to slay his son.

11. And the angel of the Lord called unto him out of heaven, and said, Abraham, Abraham: and he said, Here am I.

12. And he said, Lay not thine hand upon the lad, neither do thou any thing unto him: for now I know that thou fearest God, seeing thou hast not withheld thy son, thine only son from me.

13. And Abraham lifted up his eyes, and looked, and behold behind him a ram caught in a thicket by his horns: and Abraham went and took the ram, and offered him up for a burnt offering in the stead of his son.

14. And Abraham called the name of that place Jehovah-Jireh: as it is said to this day, In the mount of the Lord it shall be seen.

15. And the angel of the Lord called unto Abraham out of heaven the second time,

16. And said, By myself have I sworn, saith the Lord, for because thou hast done this thing, and hast not withheld thy son, thine only son:

17. That in blessing I will bless thee, and in multiplying I will multiply thy seed as the stars of the heaven, and as the sand which is upon the sea shore; and thy seed shall possess the gate of his enemies;

18. And in thy seed shall all the nations of the earth be blessed; because thou hast obeyed my voice."

Hebrews 11:17-19 "By faith Abraham, when he was tried, offered up Isaac: and he that had received the promises offered up his only begotten son, Of whom it was said, That in Isaac shall thy seed be called: Accounting that God was able to raise him up, even from the dead; from whence also he received him in a figure."

From Wikipedia: "In *The Guide for the Perplexed*, Maimonides argues that the story of the Binding of Isaac contains two "great notions." First, Abraham's willingness to sacrifice Isaac demonstrates the limit of humanity's capability to both love and fear God. Second, because Abraham acted on a prophetic vision of what God had asked him to do, the story exemplifies how prophetic revelation has the same truth value as philosophical argument and thus carries equal certainty, notwithstanding the fact that it comes in a dream or vision." (*Maimonides. The Guide of the Perplexed*, Vol. 2, Book III, Ch. 24. English translation by Shlomo Pines. Chicago: University of Chicago Press, 1963.)

Abraham was to be the founder of two lines, one through Isaac and one through Ishmael. The number of generations from Abraham to David was fourteen, from David to the carrying away to Babylon was again fourteen, and from Babylon to Jesus, again fourteen generations. *(Matthew 1:17)*

The debate on eternal good and evil will arise many times in this tome, as will references to the size and nature of the of the universe. Those with a propensity for thinking that we are not alone in the universe are the ones who will have the most fun with this line of thought.

A Note About the Bible

The Bible is the greatest book ever written on the themes of fornication, copulation, adultery, homicide, patricide, and genocide. Over many years of writing by many authors, the theme has been consistently to live a good life and work diligently to get into Heaven.

The Bible is most likely the strangest and most labyrinthine of any book of instructions you will ever encounter. The metaphors are complex. The serpent as a metaphor is just one example. God's use of metaphors to express His wisdom can be a challenge for the neophyte,

The Bible is good at double meanings. Dead and asleep are in constant use and frequently interchanged. One that is dead in Christ should be awakened. In this single sentence, both senses of the words are used.

It is illuminating to compare passages in the Bible, correlating information in one book with that of other books. One of the books that is essential in finding the parallels is *Strong's Concordance*, listed in the bibliography at the end of the book.

Finding the underlying meanings and parallels in the Bible by diligent study and being able to back up my opinions with chapter and verse is more fun to me than finding some one who claims to be a Biblical expert, and my questioning tells me they are not reading the Word itself.

Take heart. God wants you to understand the Bible. His mission is to inspire all to work and gain wisdom.

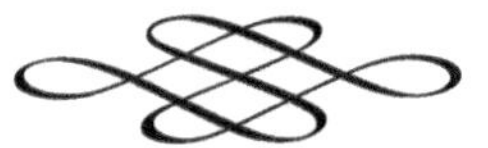

Chapter 1
In The Beginning

Your earthly soul and its relationship to your celestial soul is an underlying theme in this book. Let's take a look at the genesis of your souls. We'll start with the story of the Garden of Eden. You may take considerable umbrage at my tall tale of how these events took place. But your story will not be as beautiful as the one I spin.

For your convenience and entertainment, I will spin two tales. Take which version you like. Whichever one you choose, they each contain the same story, that of the birth of your earthly soul.

The story of the Garden of Eden has significance because it is Step One in God's plan for your education, for your gaining further knowledge of your soul.

The Almighty is responsible for the creation of Satan as well as of Adam. Does that make Lucifer and Adam brothers? If they have the same Father, they could be difficult to distinguish.

In an effort to establish a recognizable difference between Adam and Satan, the Almighty, the Boss, used an innovative tactic: having Adam pass through the birth canal and become a human being. Satan is unable to achieve this distinction. We'll get to the part about Adam passing through the birth canal when we get to his final reincarnation.

Lilith. Jewish mythology embellishes the beginning of the Bible a bit, giving Adam a concubine named Lilith who arrives on the scene prior to Eve. In Jewish lore, Lilith and Adam can only produce demons, which is unacceptable. Adam therefore needs a true love mate.   That's where Eve comes in. Satan beguiles Eve and plants a seed for Cain. Our hero Adam, returning from a long absence, does the normal thing - he also beguiles Eve. Here we have the first evidence of nature taking charge. Eve is in estrus and this time, no doubt, experiences ecstasy.

To reproduce is not a sin, but some uses of sex may not be considered acceptable, and that *would* constitute a sin. The determination of which uses are sinful and which are not is up to the individual. It's not a matter of being banned in Boston or some southern county in a state that seceded from the union.

Adam and Eve, Version One According to Bill

In the beginning God created the heavens and the Earth. Kazam! And he created Adam.

Just think of Adam as a box of dirt from the four corners of the earth, with water added. The Heavenly Potter now forms the resulting clay into this two-legged creature called Adam. After God perfects the puppet He has designed, He gives it the breath of life and he gives it a soul. That soul is a portion of the hem of God's robe. God does not literally wear a long white robe, of course. What is given to Adam and to each one of us is actually a piece of God's light, a piece of His robe of light.

God plants two trees in the middle of the Garden, the Tree of Truth and Knowledge, and the Tree of Life. There is only one law in the whole world: Do not eat, or even touch, the Tree of Truth and Knowledge or the Tree of Life. It is certain death if you violate this one rule.

The Almighty in His infinite wisdom decides that Adam should not live alone. He creates a help meet[1] (i.e. a suitable helper) for Adam. (The Almighty was in the cloning business long before modern man ever developed the technique.) God puts Adam into a deep sleep, and from a rib of Adam He forms a woman. In my imagination He creates a beautiful woman with red hair, green eyes, and a lovely body. Since she is the first, Adam names her Eve.

In the beginning, Adam and Eve, residents of the Garden, were not human because they were created by the hand of God and didn't travel through the birth

---

1   From a interpretation of the phrase in *Genesis 2:18* "an help meet" for Adam (i.e. suitable for him).

10

canal into this realm. This may sound confusing. Well, it is. We'll come back to this subject later. Adam and Eve in the Garden were naked and not yet equipped to enjoy the sex act. Adam was still just a good old angel.

This planet Earth, our galactic home, was perfect in the beginning. No smog. No traffic. And take the behavior of the animals on the great plains of Africa. With capabilities to crossbreed from cat to cat, they did not choose to do so.

Inherent in these dumb animals was the instinct to keep the lineage clean, to preserve their uniqueness so that when the future human animals came along, they would have the opportunity to observe and marvel at the biodiversity in God's world - at the beauty, for example, of an animal that could run 80 miles per hour, long before the Model T.

Adam had it pretty soft. He had the privilege and honor of naming all the animals that were the product of the Creator's fertile imagination. There were no dishes to wash, no clothes to make or mend, no floors to mop. A spirit in the spirit world, Adam had no cares.

But in the eyes of God, a serious deficiency may have existed in Adam. Such a spirit has no means or desire to gain knowledge and wisdom. God did not plan for the spirits in His domain to lack the opportunity to gain knowledge and wisdom. Hmmm. Could God dream up a diabolical scheme, a challenging obstacle course to build up the mental and spiritual muscle of the minds of His select spirits? Sure as the dickens, He could. And that's where Satan came in.

Returning to our story . . .

You see, there's a neighbor in the Garden. And this good neighbor Satan has developed the habit of visiting the beautiful lady in the Garden next door. He pays no mind that the Garden is gated. Rules, schmules. He can do without them.

Well, it's one thing and another and eventually Satan and Eve's conversation gets around to the rules that pertain to living in the Garden.

Eve remarks to the neighbor that God told Adam not to eat of the trees in the center of the Garden or he would die. The neighbor laughs at her and assures her that surely God did not intend for them to die, after all the hard work of bringing them onto the earth.

Satan convinces Eve that the fruit is indescribably delicious and encourages her to harvest a ripe fruit or two. Eve bites into the fruit, and . . . "Oh! Wow! Satan is right! This is *good!*"

This is how the neighbor beguiles Eve.

When Adam comes home from his entertaining job of naming the animals, Eve offers the fruit to him. He concurs that it is good. In all of their exuberance and joy from this good fruit, they don't notice Satan approaching as softly as the mist. The fruit tastes ever so delicious, and Eve has not previously eaten anything. Ever. All she and Adam are thinking about is this amazing flavor.

Satan has many attributes, one of them being his ability to deceive and impregnate a woman. Satan's sexual prowess is well-known and his ways are devious and sneaky. Satan has the ability to fecundate Eve easily because he is able to utilize a tiny hole in the hymen just big enough for the semen and use the tip of his tail to deposit it.

Now with his tail, Satan has just copulated with Eve. Fecundation has taken place. Neither Eve or Adam are aware of this, for Satan has not been inconvenienced by the need to pull her panties down. Eve does not have any on. In heaven there are no clothes, no kitchens, no laundries, no lingerie shops, no hair salons. There are none of the mundane distractions that man endures today.

When did this take place? Was it possible that Adam observed the event, but didn't understand what he was seeing? Or was Satan with his long tail able to perform this act so stealthily that Adam is left completely unaware?

The moment Eve ate the forbidden fruit, she became an earthling, a woman in estrus. There was no copulating in the Garden of Eden prior to Satan taking advantage of Eve.

Death came in the sense that Adam and Eve were no longer spirits: they were mortals. Their eyes were opened, and they saw that they were naked. They made aprons with fig leaves for their bodies and hid in the Garden.

In the cool of the evening, The Boss comes sashaying along on His regular walk, stopping every now and again to smell the roses.

"Adam, my boy, where are you?" God calls.

Adam responds, "Hiding in the bushes with Eve."

"Why are you hiding? Have you eaten of the forbidden fruit? Adam, my boy, why have you done this??"

Adam protests, "It was not me. It was the woman you gave me! She made me do it!"

Eve tells God it is not her fault either. *(Genesis 3:13)* It is the neighbor's fault. He has beguiled her. The Hebrew word in this passage is nasha (pronounced naw-shaw), and can not only mean seduced, but utterly deluded.

The serpent's role in this event is the role of comforter to Eve. The role of Satan as a comforter works well for Satan; it enables him to beguile Eve with ease.

The Boss turns to Eve and tells her that she has conceived. He explains that she is pregnant. Adam and Eve are ignoramuses in this field of procreation. God tells Eve that because she broke the rules, her conception will bring her pain and sorrow. Adam and Eve are not aware of this fact. *(Genesis 3:16)*

Turning to the serpent, God tells him that he will for all time crawl upon his belly. Oddly enough, the serpent eventually ends up as a healer and is revered for all time. *(John 3:14)* [Note that as Moses raised up the bronze serpent to save the Israelites from the poison snakes, so should Christ, (Adam) be raised up, to save us from eternal damnation. Christ is compared to a serpent.]

In her ignorance, Eve continues to be joyous and takes Adam to bed for more copulating. So ol' Adam "knew" (had sex with) Eve, and a second conception took place. Adam and Eve did not know that the neighbor had already planted a seed. Adam has taken the hymen in the fecundation of Eve with Abel, the baby to be.

It may seem surprising that Adam did not know that he had been cuckolded. By not breaking the hymen, Satan concealed the evidence and fooled Adam into thinking he was Eve's first. However, in *1 John 3:12-13* and again in *2 Corinthians 11:3*, it is written that Satan fathered Cain. In time, in a future reincarnation, Adam will surely figure this out.

Are you able to comprehend that Adam did not know that he had been cuckolded, until he read in *1 John 3:12* that Satan was the father of Cain? Prior to that time, Eve was a pure soul in heaven and had no knowledge of estrus, copulating, and fecundation.

Cain and Abel

In due time Eve delivers two boys, the twins Cain and Abel. They have the same mother, but different fathers. This is the world's first instance of heteropaternal superfecundation, a phenomenon that happens when two different males father fraternal twins. Although it is extremely uncommon, DNA tests done as evidence in paternity suits have shown that it does indeed happen. The *supposed* father of both boys is Adam, but we know different.

The plot is now in force. Humans have been created and delivered through the birth canal. Life here on earth as we know it is now a done deal.

Note that the Almighty does not chastise Eve too severely for her role in the eating of the fruit. In God's finely crafted plan, Eve is slated to fill a greater role in the future, one that she can't begin to imagine. The Almighty needed Eve to commit the sin in order to initiate the learning process for the heavenly souls.

Adam is a good provider, and the boys grow and wax strong. Cain chooses the life of a farmer, and Abel becomes a shepherd. The season comes for the offerings to God. Cain's sacrifice is not accepted. To his surprise, it is rejected. Abel's sacrificial offering, however, is welcomed. Stunned and infuriated by this unexpected kick in the teeth, Cain attacks his brother and slays him in the field

Cain is punished, of course. He is expelled from his homeland, lock, stock and barrel. He leaves the outer reaches of the Garden and takes on the role of a family man elsewhere. As you may have figured out, Cain is Satan's representative. Cain becomes fruitful and multiplies, increasing Satan's reach on earth.

The story of Eve's first-born twins and the struggle of good and evil is not without parallel in modern literature. *East of Eden* by John Steinbeck is an example. It is considered by many, including Steinbeck himself, to be his best work. A central theme of the book is free will, a topic we will cover later in this book.

Abel had not taken a wife by the time he suffered fratricide, so there is now no way to continue the lineage of Adam. The burden of responsibility to produce an offspring to keep the family continuing now falls to Adam and Eve. It is necessary for Adam to know Eve again, and the result of that copulation is a son, Seth. With

Abel now unable to fill the role of God's representative here on earth, Adam and Eve's third child, the newly-arrived Seth, must serve as a replacement.

It should be noted here that the entire development of the intrigue in this narrative thus far is to establish a means for the edification of the heavenly spirits. *The real reason for the existence of humans here on earth is to learn something, to increase their wisdom.*

The Cast in Act I. The four main characters in Act I of God's fancy and elaborate fairy tale are Adam, his lovely mate Eve, their son Abel, and the Evil One.

We have covered three of the important Garden scene characters and will now turn our attention to Satan.

In *Revelation 12:9*, the dragon, the serpent, the Devil and Satan are all mentioned in a single verse. Are all four of these figures one and the same, or are there four separate Satanic evildoers? The closing of the verse mentions the creature as a single figure, not four separate entities.

This confusion originates in Genesis at the eating of the forbidden fruit. The fecundation of Eve is difficult to comprehend, as the serpent would have some carnal obstacle to copulation.

Initially, there was only one Satanic figure in my picture, and with his tail he could easily have seduced Eve. No Kama Sutra instruction manual required. Just put his tail put to work and deposit the sperm. To assist in the understanding of the fecundation of Eve: Satan would be there to do the work of seduction, and God could call him a serpent, sliding through the grass, silent, and crafty. It may be that God wants to let Satan know that he is to grovel in the face of God and man.

Revelation 12:4 also mentions a great red dragon, a dragon who stands ready to devour a child the minute it is delivered by a certain woman. The baby is born and immediately ascends to the throne of God, where the child is safe.

But here's the problem with the image of the evil serpent as portrayed in the story of the tree in the midst of the Garden. Later on in the Bible we find that the serpent is not the bad creature as pictured. The serpent also has healing qualities.

In the desert God introduced some serpents to bite the Israelites. They had fallen out of grace, and He punished them with snakes. The people protested and complained, so God had Moses make a symbol of a bronze snake entwined on a staff. He was to raise this up in the midst of the people as a sign. Those who were bitten could look upon the snake be healed. In *John 3:14*, Christ would be raised as the serpent was raised. The serpent in these passages is a healer and savior, joined with Christ.

Does *Revelation 12:9* explain that Satan was the neighbor? There is another verse in which Satan as a roaring lion goes about seeing who he may devour. Satan is slated to fill many roles in his obsession to keep in his possession all the souls he corralled out of heaven.

With the arrival of Seth, the curtain comes down on Act I.

There are a myriad of stories in the Bible, and these four characters will be presented in the stories as required to provide this author's evidence that the Old Testament writes the New Testament. The number of stories that will be generated from these four characters is beyond imagining.

The Main Characters and Their Relationships

Father God	Son Adam
Father Adam	Son Abel
Elijah (Adam reincarnated)	Elisha (Abel reincarnated)
Christ (Adam reincarnated)	John the Baptist (Abel reincarnated)
Christ Savior	Holy Ghost (John the Baptist reincarnated)
Grand Dad (God)	Grandson (Abel)

Chapter 2
Plan B From Outer Space

The Bible is rife with metaphors. If there's any book that illustrates that there's more than one way to explain things, it's the Bible. For your amusement, and perhaps to shake your brain loose from conventional thinking, here's my own alternative version of the Adam and Eve story.

In the beginning God created the heavens and the earth. Considering the infinite size of this universe, it would not really be too farfetched to entertain the idea that there had already been some substantial creating going on, and that there could be other rocks orbiting other stars, like Rigel in the constellation Orion. It is not too improbable that some of those faraway rocks might have creatures on them.

So why would it be surprising if Adam and Eve arrived here on good old planet Earth from somewhere else? Their modern means of transportation would be filled with the tools and materials for building cities. Let's follow their travels.

Right now they are just coming into South America, following the path laid out on the high plateau. This is not their first pleasure trip to this lovely planet. But this time they are here to put down roots and build a planet of people. Adam and Eve discover the Garden of Eden and choose it for their ideal new home. The Garden is full of lovely trees, with fruit and nuts, and there are also animals for food.

Time passes, and one day the Old Man comes into the Garden, strolling in the cool of the evening. He sees Adam and Eve. Approaching them with caution, He

The Nazca Lines are a series of ancient geoglyphs located in the Nazca Desert in southern Peru. They were designated as a UNESCO World Heritage Site in 1994. The high, arid plateau stretches more than 80 km (50 mi) between the towns of Nazca and Palpa on the Pampas de Jumana about 400 km south of Lima. Although some local geoglyphs resemble Paracas motifs, scholars believe the Nazca Lines were created by the Nazca culture between 400 and 650 AD. The hundreds of individual figures range in complexity from simple lines to stylized hummingbirds, spiders, monkeys, fish, sharks, orcas, and lizards.

The designs are shallow lines made in the ground by removing the reddish pebbles and uncovering the whitish/grayish ground beneath. Hundreds are simple lines or geometric shapes; more than 70 are zoomorphic designs of animals such as birds, fish, llamas, jaguars, monkeys, or human figures. Other designs include phytomorphic shapes such as trees and flowers. The largest figures are over 200 m (660 ft) across. Scholars differ in interpreting the purpose of the designs, but in general, they ascribe religious significance to them.

Due to its isolation and to the dry, windless, and stable climate of the plateau, the lines have mostly been naturally preserved. Extremely rare changes in weather may temporarily alter the general designs. As of recent years, the lines are said to have been deteriorating due to an influx of squatters inhabiting the lands.

Wikipedia

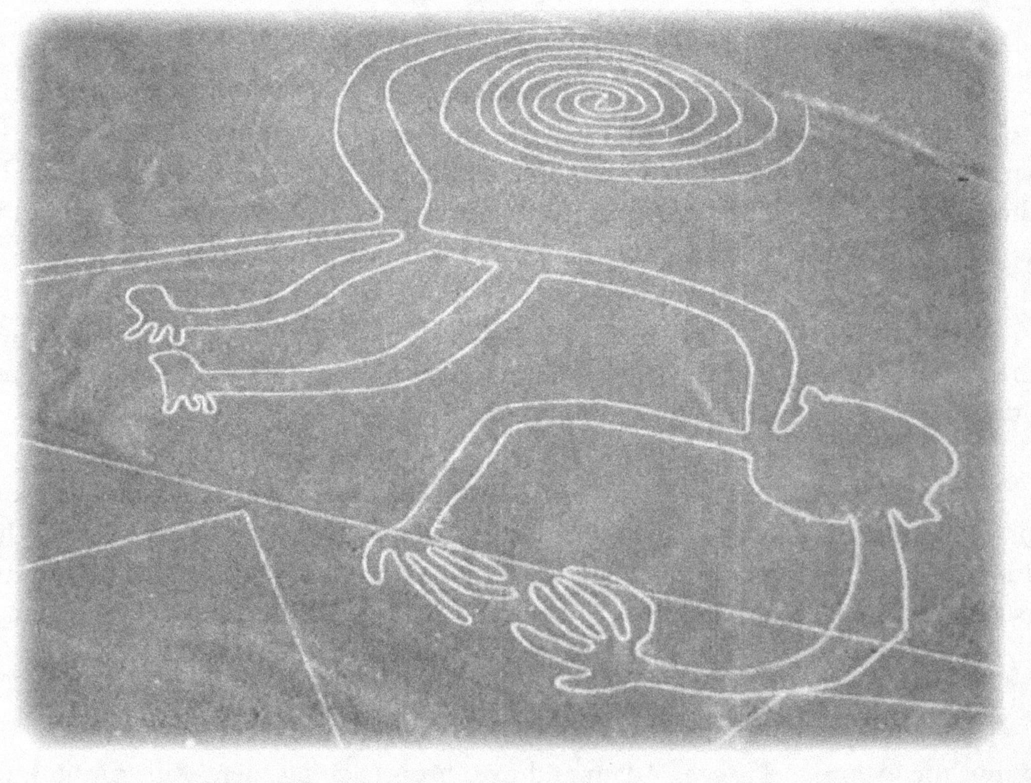

asks Adam, who are you? Adam replies that he and his help meet are from a planet in the vicinity of Rigel in the constellation of Orion.

Adam informs The Almighty that they have been here before and are now returning to inhabit this planet. In a lengthy conversation, God shares with them the details of all the work He has done in creating this Garden. Adam is quite impressed and admires its beauty.

"There is one rule," The Almighty tells Adam. "It is simple. There are two trees in the middle of the Garden. One is the Tree of Truth and Knowledge, and the other is the Tree of Life. You are more than welcome to stay here, but you are not allowed to touch, prune, or eat of the fruit of these trees."

Adam is pleased with the knowledge that they can remain here in the Garden, and live off the land - and with the Owner's permission to boot!

With all this glorious and wonderful environment, time slips by quickly. The Owner comes by for a chat from time to time. One day, however, another individual saunters nonchalantly up the path. Adam, recognizing that this is not the owner, goes up to the intruder and inquires who he might be. Now Satan, rather hard to miss in his red suit, long forked tail, and the horned head says, "I am Lucifer."

"So what do you do here on earth?" Adam asks this new friend. "Oh," Satan replies, "I'm the top executive; I'm in charge and have a third of the Universe's souls to rule over." Adam looks taken aback. So to put Adam in an easier mood, Satan adds, "Just kidding. I am only your neighbor down the road." Having created a cheerful friendship, Satan trots on home.

In the next day or so, the Owner comes by again, enjoying the cool of the evening, and asks if Adam would be interested in the job of creating names for all the animals. Adam likes the opportunity. When Adam asks the Owner if He had at any time offered this job to Adam's neighbor, the Almighty replies that they are not friendly.

The Almighty asks Adam about transportation for the job, as Adam will need to get around to all the different locations on the planet. Adam replies, "Not a problem, Boss. "There's the ship we came here in. It works fine."

The Almighty is pleased with the new arrival. Adam is approved for the job. He can name the animals. After a couple of months spent naming the animals in the Garden and vicinity, it comes time to travel outside of the Garden to work on the names of the rest. The trip to Australia is especially interesting. For one thing, there is a beaver-like animal with the face of a duck and another animal with a handy built-in pocket.

Eve enjoys the traveling, but on some occasions she stays in the Garden. Adam doesn't like to leave her alone, but the neighbor in the red suit says, "Not to worry, pal," and then generously offers to come over while Adam is gone and check up on the attractive lady with the red hair and green eyes.

Keeping his promise while Adam is out of town, the neighbor becomes a frequent visitor. He says that he feels responsible for checking on Eve and making sure that she is doing fine and not in any need while her husband is out of town.

Their friendly conversations lead to a discussion of the two trees that Adam and Eve are not to touch. Eve explains that eating the forbidden fruit will kill them. The neighbor makes her feel silly and foolish for believing such a preposterous fairy tale, considering how advanced her home planet is. Eve tries some of the fruit. Not only does she not die, but the fruit is indescribably delicious.

A few days later, Adam comes home. Eve takes some of the fruit of the Tree of Truth and Knowledge and gives it to Adam. The two of them agree that it is excellent. But sure as Murphy's Law, the Owner shows up for His evening walk. Adam suddenly notices that he and Eve are naked and hurries Eve to a hiding spot. The Owner cries out, "Adam, where are you?" Adam responds, "We are naked and hiding ourselves over here in this patch of poison oak."

"Adam? Did you eat of the forbidden trees?" Adam stammers, "The neighbor told Eve that we would not die from eating this fruit. Eve picked some of the fruit, and we ate it. It's not my fault!"

Unknown to either Adam or Eve, the neighbor has made a deposit in Eve and she is pregnant. She is also in estrus for the first time and takes Adam to bed. She conceives two sons by two different fathers, one by Satan and one by Adam. The boys Cain and Abel are born.

There is now a caucus of four individuals, Adam and Eve, Cain and Abel. The Owner is still in charge and condemns the sinners. The Owner tells the serpent he will grovel and crawl in the dust for all time for assisting Satan in the beguiling of Eve. They are all banished from the Garden. Guards are put on the gates, and the family is now living in a new place where they actually have to work. Adam is the supposed father of both of the boys, but in truth he only fathered Abel. The second baby, Cain, will multiply the seed of Satan.

Cain is filled with envy when his brother one-ups him in a religious ritual. Unfortunately for Abel, Cain has an anger management issue, loses his temper, and kills his brother. Banished from the area as punishment, Cain takes a wife in a distant land. In this new land, Cain builds a great city, using the tools that were in the space ship with Adam and Eve.

In the meantime, in order to preserve the lineage of Adam, Eve gives birth to Seth.

Is this taking away something from your Sunday School lessons about the first story in the Bible? That is not my intention here. My aim is showing that there are different ways of explaining the same situation.

Whichever story you choose, it is an entry into understanding the concept of your two souls: you celestial soul and your earthly soul.

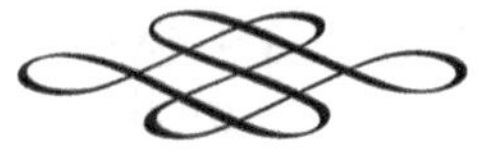

Chapter 3
The Terrestrial and Celestial Soul

The concept of the soul is very interesting. Over the millennia, volumes have been written on the topic by sages from Aristotle and Socrates to Thomas Aquinas to modern philosophers. Almost every one of these writers agrees that there is something about us that no one can quite put a finger on. In my opinion, based on a great deal of study, that "certain something" is our soul. In fact, not only do we each have a soul. We each have *two*.

When God created Adam, it was paramount that Adam have a soul. This was accomplished when the Almighty breathed life into Adam. In modern Judaism the soul is believed to be given by God to each person upon their first breath, as described in Genesis, "And the LORD God formed man of the dust of the ground, and breathed into his nostrils the breath of life; and man became a living being." *(Genesis 2:7)*

Adam was not real flesh at this time; Adam was spirit. Notice that we are not told that Adam was consuming food from any part of the Garden. Spirits do not require substance for existence. When Eve was brought into the picture, she was given a soul. Where do these souls come from? They are a part of the hem of God's robe, a part of anything that is God's, and all of it is the property of the Almighty. What you desire to think that your soul is made of is up to you.

Two souls in every body. Lets investigate the idea of the presence of two souls in every body, an earthly soul and a celestial soul. The heavily traveled trail from here to heaven and back by many individuals provides the evidence to all who can read. So do the near death experiences that so many people have had.

At this point in our trip, the mental journey may not be what you anticipated. The idea of two souls may seem very farfetched. Is there a Biblical basis for this? Consider the passage in which Jesus says, ". . . and other sheep I have, which are not of this fold, and they shall hear my voice." The sheep are a metaphor for our souls. The two folds are the heavenly fold and the earthly fold. Understanding the meaning of the two folds, and the bringing together of the them, is the zenith that we pursue in these lines. *(John 10:14-16)*

We begin with the book of Revelation and the account of the separation of the heavenly host. It is written that Satan, with his long whip tail, lassoed one third of the heavenly host, leaving two thirds in Heaven with the Father.

Revelation 12:3-4 introduces the reader to a bad and terrible dragon, (aka Satan) who with a sweep of his tail removes a third of the stars, i.e. the souls, from heaven.

Revelation 12:9 is very explicit: the souls have been banished to Earth. Earth becomes home to the exiled souls, but two thirds of the souls remain in heaven with the Father. There are additional passages elsewhere on the souls. However, for this narrative we will use only the evidence from the Book of John and the Book of Revelation. It is important that you read all of the account in John, describing the souls, as well as the account in Revelation of the taking of the souls.

Why did God allow Satan to take all these souls? The answer is education. With no stress, there is no learning. And when all was perfect for the heavenly host, there was no stress.. Earth and the laws of nature were not problems. The lions stayed with their strain, as also did the dinosaurs. The monkeys and the apes did not mix. The plants grew without a gardener.

The Almighty called in Lucifer. Together they laid out a plan that would give the souls the opportunity to gain greatly in wisdom and understanding. The Archangel Michael was called forth. The Almighty instructed Michael to throw Lucifer out of heaven. (God was not about to share His throne with anyone else anyway.) The Almighty had created Lucifer, so He was able to make Lucifer do anything that God desired. This meant sending Lucifer to earth to be in charge.

Lucifer needed a following, so they arranged for Lucifer to take a third of the heavenly host for his own host down here on earth. This host is now here on earth with Satan, looking up to the Evil One and doing his bidding. The Satanic followers have been able to make excellent use of all the good things that the Almighty has created. They have free will, and can follow the dictates of whichever leader they wish.

The gift of free will means that they are able to use the Creator's fabrication in any manner they choose. Their earthly leader once even inveigled them into building a tower in the city of Babel that would reach to Heaven. It was the best place to live. Everyone who was anyone wanted to move there. The Almighty didn't like their hubris or their speaking a single language because that meant they would become too powerful. Consequently, He came down and scrambled up the languages. That stopped *that* project.

This is where the fun in the study begins. Did the Almighty Father create this complicated plotline for a purpose? My take on it is that in order for His souls in heaven to learn something, there had to be a challenging educational program. There had to be a dialectical conflict between good and evil that would provide an opportunity to make choices and to exercise free will.

There are additional avenues of learning that are full of mirth and fun. It is now clear to me that God is not as mean as my previous thinking had me believing. He wants to share my mirth, on earth and in Heaven. Take up the cross and have a good time.

The Earthly Soul and the Heavenly Soul. To clarify the nature of the two souls in the earthling's body: The soul from heaven is the celestial soul, and it cannot be lured into the snares of Satan.

In *John 10*, Jesus goes into great detail on how this works. He is the shepherd, and His sheep know His voice. The important point is that these sheep cannot be taken from Him. They cannot be lured away. In the Garden of Eden, Satan did take Adam and Eve from the heavenly fold, and they became earthlings.

The soul as the voice within cannot and will not lose its place in heaven. St. Thomas Aquinas says the unborn baby receives this soul forty days after conception. That's when the voice within is activated.

The terrestrial soul is also selected. The book of Revelation describes how Satan is allowed to gather followers. The Almighty does not stop this thievery. My study of the Bible leads me to think that God and Lucifer are in this educational program together. Having free will is important in understanding belief and the path to paradise.

The Souls. There is a reason for this journey that you are undertaking. The Christ tells the world that He has many mansions in heaven. Your job is to gain knowledge and experience (empirical wisdom) that will enable you to rise into the realm of a loftier mansion. You will do this by listening to the *voice within.*

The Voice Within. The following Biblical quotes relate to the building and destruction of the temple, to the gift of manual skill, and the value of men of wisdom, i.e. those who have learned to listen to the voice within:

Exodus 31:3 "And I have filled him with the spirit of God, in wisdom, and in understanding, and in knowledge, and in all manner of workmanship." Along the same lines are *Exodus 35:31, Exodus 35:35, Exodus 36:1,* and *1 Kings 10:7*

Acts 6:3 "Wherefore, brethren, look ye out among you seven men of honest report, full of the Holy Ghost and wisdom, whom we may appoint over this business." In this context, I read "full of the Holy Ghost" as listening to the voice within.

Matthew 11:19 "The Son of man came eating and drinking, and they say, Behold a man gluttonous, and a winebibber, a friend of publicans and sinners. But wisdom is justified of her children."

Luke 7:35 "But wisdom is justified of all her children."

These are the works describing your skills to be used here on earth, but there is also the wisdom you acquire from the voice within to keep you steadfast with the Almighty. *If you are in need of help in keeping steadily on the path of enlightenment, the Holy Ghost will come to you as the Voice Within.*

Two Divergent Sources of Souls, Cain and Seth. Here things get a bit complicated. Lucifer and Adam are brothers. They share the same father, God. Interestingly, they also end up sharing the same woman, Eve. One sexual encounter provides the sperm for Cain, and the other sexual encounter, the sperm for Abel.

Now there are two divergent sources of souls. One line of people is in the lineage of Cain, and the other is in the lineage of Seth.

We get to *Genesis, Chapter 6* and we find that the sons of God looked upon the daughters of men and liked what they saw. The followers of Satan, the lineage of Cain, were also beautiful. *(Genesis 6:2–4)* Some of God's followers found the girls on earth pleasing to look at and took some to wife. This was displeasing to God. These sons of Satan produced giants in those times, men of renown. The lineage of Seth also had pretty girls here on earth. This intermixing with the sons and daughters of Satan's following was also a problem for God. God thought that if He could find some whose lineage was purely of Seth, He could wipe out all of whom He did not approve.

Because the Almighty was not pleased with mankind, He caused the great flood. This reduced the lineage of Cain and Seth to the sons of Noah. Since we now no longer harbor a true lineage because it is possible that the sons of Noah may have either Cain souls or Seth souls. This is probably the advent of free will. And the likelihood is that with the advent of free will, it was now up to the individual to decide if he wants to be chosen or not to be chosen. *(Matthew 20:16)* "So the last shall be first, and the first last: for many be called, but few chosen."

At this point, the Bible does not go into any great length about Abel and the role he ultimately played out in the story. However, he is mentioned again in lessons in the New Testament. *(1 John 3:12 and Hebrews 11:4)* We'll return to Abel when we get to the section on reincarnation.

Belief and Free Will. Free will is an important idea in the Bible. The fact that you choose how you will interpret the entire biblical text is tantamount to having free will. Free will requires that you have a belief and think through the assumptions based on that belief and their consequences. You may believe in evolution, but I have no concrete evidence that it is any more the real thing than my belief in creation. Having a belief is necessary for the gaining of the Celestial Spark.

The writers Raymond A. Moody, Michael Newton, Pim Van Lommel, and Eben Alexander all proclaim that there is more to life than what we experience here on earth. That is the first step in gaining the Celestial Spark. Observe your ears (more on ears in another chapter) in the mirror, and you will have some good knowledge as to how many times you have had an opportunity to gain the Spark. It is time to make a free will decision. Gain wisdom and understanding. Why not? *Ignite your investigative mode.*

In *John 3:22–27*, The disciples of John The Baptist and Christ ask if Christ is the real thing, or is John still the one with the power? The answer to the question is not clear from the reading of the passages. The rascal that had this Bible composed has made a point of leaving the door open for you to decide. It is free will at work.

Job 33:26-33 talks about bringing back the soul to the light; the passage contrasts the terrestrial soul and the celestial soul. The reference to bringing the soul back from the pit refers to redeeming the earthly body and soul. God is trying to reclaim as many souls as He can from Satan.

Free will plays an important part, leaving the choice up to the individual. In verse 31, Job is beseeched to listen to the voice within. In the last verse, the inner voice tells Job to listen, and he will learn wisdom.

In *Leviticus 4:2*, the writer is referring to the earthly soul. The soul from heaven cannot sin. The voice within is wisdom and truth. *Leviticus 4* goes into great detail about what the sinning soul must do to be cleansed. This illustrates the action that must take place to confess and show repentance.

Other passages that dwell on the heavenly soul and the earthly soul are:
Psalm 23: The shepherd is a metaphor for the soul within.
Psalm 25:12: God will teach you the way that you should choose.
Psalm 25:14: The Lord will provide instruction

If you learn to hear the voice, you will not fall into Satan's trap. If you do not hear the voice, Satan will have you. Let us take a closer look at the perils of life here on earth. The Almighty instructs you and your earthly body to be fruitful and multiply. Oh my! Built-in temptation! And this is okay?? Will you enjoy some pleasure in producing one of these evil characters here on earth? From the passages, it is true that God says to be fruitful and multiply.

Now appears the wisdom that can grow out of fecundation and the joy of copulation, the dark side of which is the sin of fornication and adultery. Why would the Almighty resort to such a lesson plan? Because the value of learning from the trials and tribulations of sin will not be recognized without the experience of actually being in the arena with sin; this creates a training ground to develop wisdom to overcome the sin.

The value of God's use of temptation as a learning tool is illustrated in the story of Abraham and Isaac in *Genesis 22:1* and further explained in *1 Corinthians 10:13*.

There's a beautiful poem by Mary Stevenson (1896 – 1985), an Australian community activist. Her poem has been used as the basis for countless sermons. Here's how I imagine the story in her poem applied to my own life.

Bill is talking with Jesus about the footprints he sees in the sand. Bill says that he has seen two sets of footprints at times, but at other times he has only seen one. Bill says that he thinks that Jesus is not with him at those times. Jesus responds that there was only one set because He was carrying Bill when he was too weak to walk.

Jesus is always there. If you are listening to the voice within, Jesus gets to walk, and if you are not listening, then He will carry you. How far and how long will He carry us?

When an offense like murder is the work you are allowing your temple to do, you are falling down on your job of keeping this earthly body on the right track. You have allowed Satan to take over your body, which is your temple here on earth. Are you to be thrown out of heaven? Not by my understanding of the operation. But you will be lowered in the level of the mansion that you had aspired to reside in.

To review, Christ as the good shepherd is described in *John 10*. In this portion of the book of John, Christ describes two flocks of sheep. One flock is already His and the other He is striving to gain in order to join it with the flock He already has. The sheep that He already has, that no man can take from Him, are guarded by His Father. These sheep represent the heavenly host; the host that provides the voice within.

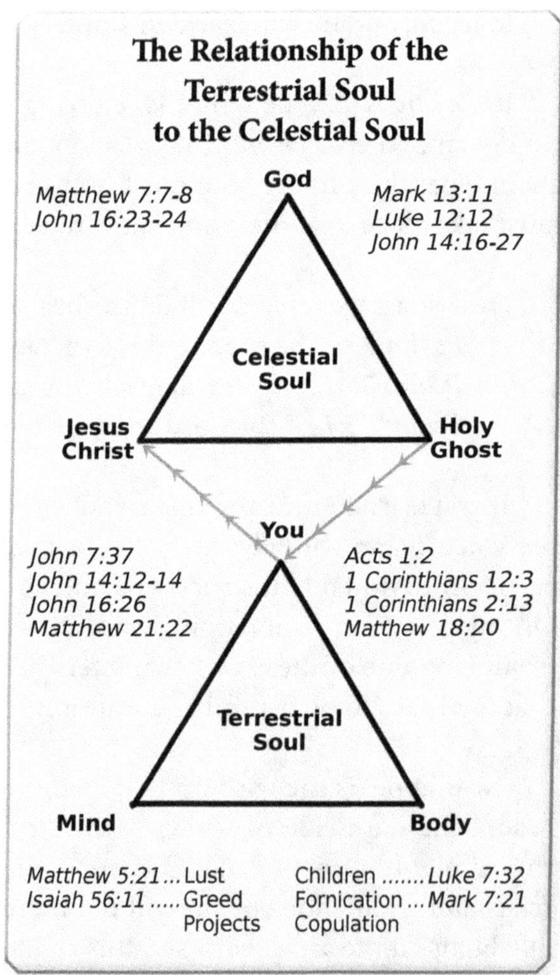

Interestingly enough, this revelation about gaining wisdom has been given to men who are not considered Christian. God seems to have a penchant for giving some great revelation to someone who is not associated with this line of thought. The three recipients that I refer to here all have a doctor's degree. This poor soul takes it on good faith that the story they tell is assuredly correct.

Thomas Aquinas, voicing his thoughts on how this all works, gives the soul from the heavenly host forty days to take on the role of the voice in this temple on earth. Thomas felt that this time frame would relieve a host soul of the unhappy situation in which a baby should happen to die shortly after the soul had entered the temple. Verses on the earthly body as a temple are found in *1 Corinthians 3:16, 2 Corinthians 6:16,* and *John 2:21.*

This part of the narrative is even more strange. The Bible states repeatedly that this earthly flesh is full of sin. The earthly soul is part of the host that the Evil One drew off from the heavenly host with his tail. *(Revelation 12:3-4)* These souls follow him here on earth. This earthly soul is composed of the mind and body.

A diagram of this information will help the neophyte to better comprehend that there are two souls in this earthly body: good and evil. The good soul from the heavenly host is lodged in this temple here on earth to strive to be heard as the voice within, to help the earthling to follow his good example.

The Voice Within

Have you ever felt that you had a voice within? You may have thought of that voice as your conscience. Where can you find information about that voice, so that you may better understand what it is? *Matthew 10:19-20* is relevant: "But when they deliver you up, take no thought how or what ye shall speak: for it shall be given you in that same hour what ye shall speak. For it is not ye that speak, but the Spirit of your Father which speaketh in you."

That the voice within is bigger than the idea of a conscience is evidenced in the creative arts. Many artists, writers, and musicians will tell you that when they are in the process of creating a book, a work of art, or a piece of music, they experience the overwhelming feeling that something outside of themselves is guiding their hand, that the creativity is not from *themselves,* but from something higher and more universal than their individuality. Something is flowing through them, and they are simply a conduit. Julia Cameron, author of *The Artist's Way, Faith and Will,* and many other works on the intersection of art and faith, has described this phenomenon well. Many of her books contain exercises on how to tap into this voice within, coming from your celestial soul.

The voice within lives in this body, referred to as the earthly temple for the heavenly spirit. *1 Corinthians 3:16* makes it very clear that you are the temple, and the spirit of God lies within. *Corinthians 17* goes on to explain that this evil earthly body is also the temple where the spirit from heaven dwells, for the duration of the life of that body here on earth.

John 16:13 explains that the Holy Ghost hears God's instructions and will guide you through the voice within:

"Howbeit when he, the Spirit of truth, is come, he will guide you into all truth: for he shall not speak of himself; but whatsoever he shall hear, that shall he speak: and he will shew you things to come."

In reference to listening to the voice within, there is a saying that "he knows in his heart the correct thing to do." It has become clear in the lessons that the voice is not in your heart but in your liver. As the liver is the cleanser of the body, the soul is the cleanser of the mind and body. You, as the heavenly soul, are charged with bringing home this earthling, that was swept away by Satan's tail.

The Order of the Souls. The time has come in this diatribe to fix the order of the souls. As you will remember, God has two thirds and Satan has one third. Mathematically, the good ones outnumber the bad at two to one. Therefore, the good should win. Unfortunately, Satan has many tools at his disposal and is well-armed. This makes it very difficult for the voice within the earthling's mind to receive the rules of God. Satan has jammed the receiver.

These next verses are intended as instructions for the earthly body, ways to develop the voice within of the soul from heaven.

In *1 Kings, Chapter 17*, the voice within Elijah told him to go Zarephath to be sustained by a widow in the days of drought. In verses *17-24*, the widow's son falls deathly ill. Elijah listens to his inner voice while caring for the son, and the heavenly soul comes back to the boy, who revives.

Our dual natures are described in *Romans 7:14–25*, especially in verse *14:* one is the law from God through the voice within, and the other is the carnal mind. This chapter illustrates the drama of the heavenly soul battling with the body and mind to follow the heavenly soul's instructions. Verse *18* makes it clear that the mind is flesh, in contrast to the voice within, which hears the voice of God and is spiritual.

The voice within is the law. The truth of this may not make it the very first time this reading is finished. The most important information is gained from the study of the voice within and how far back in history it is recorded. The Egyptians, with their strong reverence for the life hereafter, stored up goods in the tombs for the individual to have in the next life.

Today there are several writers and researchers keeping records of people leaving this earth and returning with a heavenly story. The average layman will not be able to understand this just from reading the Bible. The neophyte requires outside information.

Three doctors have written books on the subject of souls in heaven and near-death experiences: Cardiologist Pim Van Lommel, MD; Neurologist Eben Alexander, MD; and Michael Newton, Ph.D. (See bibliography.)

You doubters will now learn that your God has an ornery streak. When He selects someone to write a lengthy presentation on His behalf, the person He selects may be someone that it will be difficult for you to accept.

Take the Apostle Paul. He's the last person you would think appropriate to relay God's message. He was a Christian killer before he saw Christ and became a Christian himself. Reading further, you will find that Paul had a wife and two sons. It was difficult to convince the apostles Peter and James to accept the Christ-appointed Saul, this family man now renamed Paul, as an apostle.

1 Corinthians 1:27-28 makes it very clear that the things of God are foolishness to man. It behooves you to read all of *1 Corinthians 1:18-31*. *1 Corinthians 3:18-21* again tells us that the wisdom of God is foolishness to man. "For the wisdom of this world is foolishness with God. For it is written, He taketh the wise in their own craftiness."

1 Corinthians 15:40 spells out that the flesh is terrestrial; the spirit is celestial. With your reading of some of the layman's books on the heavenly souls, you will get a better understanding of why the souls are sent to dwell in this earthly body. You, the heavenly soul, are here to strive to get the earthly mind to adhere to your instructions from the heavenly Father, through the Holy Ghost.

Noah had a spirit in him from the beginning. Like the rest of us, the most difficult thing to overcome arose from his heavenly soul residing in his earthling body, the heavenly soul's earth temple. The challenge was to make the earthly body and mind adhere to and follow the instructions from the Holy Ghost, as revealed through the voice within.

The ark had settled down, and Noah had started to cultivate the land. He had planted some grape vines. After consuming too much of the nectar from the fruit of the vine, he fell asleep. The son Ham saw his father's naked body, and this act on his part was a grave sin. The other two brothers covered their eyes, not to see their father in this state, and they covered Noah. Like Noah, our biggest challenge is often getting our earthly body to obey the voice within.

Take comfort in the message of the psalms of David. To better understand the voice within, we will look at the twenty-third Psalm. (In my opinion, *The Catholic New American Bible* translation of this Psalm is the closest to visualizing the earthly body and the soul within.) The Biblical text below is from the King James Version of the Christian Bible; it is in the public domain.

"The Lord is my shepherd, I shall not want." The psalmist in the first line states that he is following his shepherd; he needs nothing more.

"He maketh me to lie down in green pastures; he leadeth me beside the still waters." The shepherd provides a safe place for His sheep, a place where the sheep have the freedom to wander about.

"He restoreth my soul: he leadeth me in the paths of righteousness for his name's sake." You, the psalmist, could take another path, but you do not. You listen and follow the shepherd because He knows the way.

"Yea, though I walk through the valley of the shadow of death, I will fear no evil: for thou art with me; thy rod and thy staff they comfort me." When the psalmist goes through some dark times, he sticks with the shepherd. If he falls into a chasm, the shepherd will rescue him with his rod and his staff. If he is attacked by wild animals, the shepherd will protect him. The rod and staff are the ones from Moses and Aaron. When Aaron threw down his rod, it ate the enemy's snakes.

"Thou preparest a table before me in the presence of mine enemies: thou anointest my head with oil; my cup runneth over." Enemies, like vipers, are present even in green pastures. The shepherd prepares a place to eat, a table, in the presence of the sheep's enemies. The custom in Biblical times was to anoint someone's head to honor and dignify him. So even you, the shepherd's charge, will be honored and dignified.

"Surely goodness and mercy shall follow me all the days of my life: and I will dwell in the house of the Lord forever." Your shepherd feeds you and anoints your head with oil. Your shepherd loves you. If you continue, you will dwell in the House of the Lord forever and ever.

In *John 10:16* Christ says, "Other sheep I have not of this fold, and I must bring them in, and they will hear my voice." When *you* hear the voice, hopefully, you will then receive the Spark.

You have a physical body here on earth, and it will stay here on earth. It never will enter the kingdom of heaven. Reports of near death experiences seem to be evidence of this premise. But your celestial soul will return to its home in Heaven.

Changes in Eve. The changes Eve endured after eating the fruit of the forbidden tree were tremendous. The soul God had given her was now separated from the first connection, and Eve had a new earthly soul consisting of her mind and body. The earthly body is the temple for the soul she had originally had. This new role for the original, celestial soul is the voice within.

The beautiful verse *Luke 1:15* is an indication that some individuals have more of the Spirit when they arrive here on earth than others. You are of good spirit, for example, if when you are given too much change, you do not keep the change. You return the change without the least equivocation or slightest hesitation.

At the other end of the spectrum is finders keepers. However, I think there is an opening, a space between the person who keeps the change and the one who returns it. Suppose you arrive home and discover that you were given too much change. Do you drive back two hundred miles, or even twenty miles to return the money?

Tough decision. This ol' codger does not judge. My advice is that as you go through life, when a difficult situation is encountered, just walk away. There are plenty of opportunities to be good. Do *not* go around the world thinking that you can make it all good. Christ did not try, and he had the power of the Almighty. You do not have any of that power.

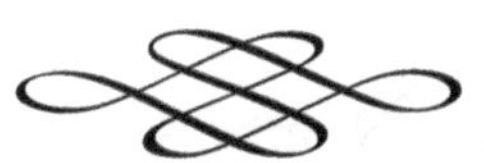

Chapter 4
Numerology, The Bible, and Freemasonry

The beginning of understanding is numerology. Patterns of numbers underlie physics, chemistry, engineering, biology. Those patterns underlie the fabric of the universe.

The Bible is full of numbers. They aren't just random. They all have a meaning in the context in which they appear. Included in this book is the story of Christ feeding the multitudes and chiding the disciples for their lack of understanding of the significance of the numbers involved.

Those individuals who accept the challenge of gaining the Celestial Spark must begin their studies in this higher realm of feelings with numerology. When you have grasped that there are transcendental numbers, such as π (pi) (3.141590), the picture will become clearer. Or when you learn to appreciate ϕ (phi), also known as the Golden Mean or the Golden Ratio, since it underlies so much of what we find beautiful in nature, like the shell of a nautilus or the arrangement of scales in a pine cone. Or when you learn about the fraction of twenty two over seven, as the base arithmetic for the perimeter of a circle. That was discovered about six thousand years ago. David Wilcock, in his book *The Source Field Investigations*, follows the concept that this advancement in knowledge comes to more than one individual at the same time.

Freemasonry and Numbers. Numbers are also of great significance in the Masonic Temple. In my own initiation into Freemasonry, there were some steps of three and five in stairs as part of the charge. There were three candles around the altar, representing the Master and Senior and Junior Wardens.

The EAD (Entered Apprentice) in Freemasonry is encouraged to memorize the opening and closing rites of the Lodge. Memorization is a good practice for the new Mason. It prepares him to grasp the real meanings of the initiation lectures, which have to do with numbers and geometry.

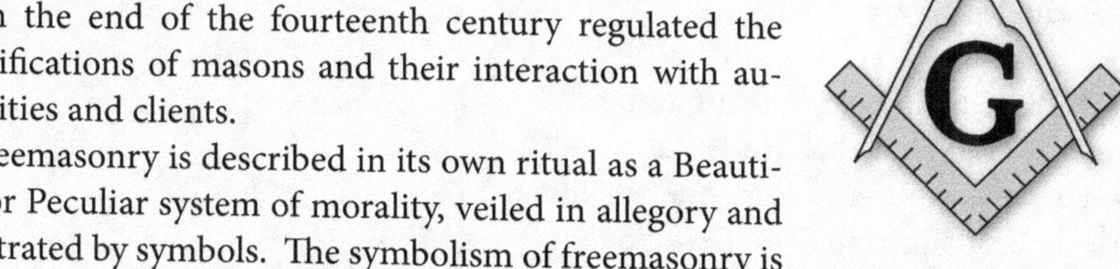

Freemasonry is a fraternal organization that traces its origins to the local fraternities of stonemasons, which from the end of the fourteenth century regulated the qualifications of masons and their interaction with authorities and clients.

Freemasonry is described in its own ritual as a Beautiful or Peculiar system of morality, veiled in allegory and illustrated by symbols. The symbolism of freemasonry is found throughout the Masonic Lodge, and contains many of the working tools of a medieval or renaissance stonemason. The whole system is transmitted to initiates through the medium of Masonic ritual, which consists of lectures and allegorical plays.

The Masonic Lodge is the basic organizational unit of Freemasonry. The bulk of Masonic ritual consists of degree ceremonies. Candidates for Freemasonry are progressively initiated into Freemasonry, first in the degree of Entered Apprentice. Some time later, in a separate ceremony, they will be passed to the degree of Fellowcraft, and finally they will be raised to the degree of Master Mason. In all of these ceremonies, the candidate is entrusted with passwords, signs and grips peculiar to his new rank.

The first Grand Lodge, the Grand Lodge of London and Westminster (later called the Grand Lodge of England (GLE)), was founded on 24 June 1717. The earliest known American lodges were in Pennsylvania. The Premier Grand Lodge of England appointed a Provincial Grand Master for North America in 1731, based in Pennsylvania.

After the American Revolution, independent U.S. Grand Lodges formed themselves within each state. Some thought was briefly given to organizing an overarching "Grand Lodge of the United States," with George Washington (who was a member of a Virginian lodge) as the first Grand Master, but the idea was short-lived. The various state Grand Lodges did not wish to diminish their own authority by agreeing to such a body.

Wikipedia

Phrases used every day expose hidden esoteric connections. Behind the eight ball, for example, is related to being in back of the number eight, which in numerology is the old twins, good and evil. In his heart the EAD knows that the voice within is talking to the earthling. The dues receipt, a good memory of the cipher, and a Shriner's jacket are not the makings of a true and accepted Mason. Numerology is the only key to achieving higher thinking.

There is much more to numerology than space allows in this volume. I suggest that you read a few of the many books available on the subject.

What the Numbers Signify

ONE. One is not really a number. It is unity. God says that He is All in All. The Hebrew word *echad* or "one" in this sense is best illustrated in *Deuteronomy 6:4*, which is a prayer that is central to the Judaic Shabbat service. *One* signifies unity, and in this verse, it expresses the concept of *compound unity*. *Adonai echad:* He is Himself, the bright light, and all that He has created. That is the essence of God. There is no Number One; He is ALL.

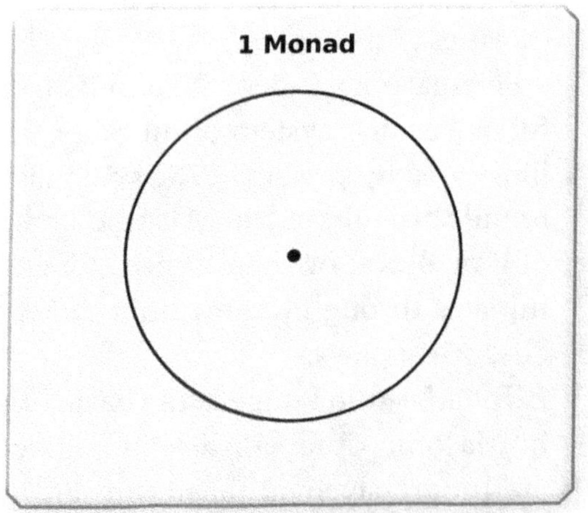

TWO. The number two is often referred to as audacity. It has the audacious distinction of cutting, parting, making different from *All*. The mission of number two is to break up the One. Who had the audacity to part the original One?

Two is very important in nature, religion, politics, and everyday life. Think of the number two as the necessary balance required in all things: Up and down, in and out, good and evil, male and female, predator and prey. It is necessary to the balance of nature, as ecologists so often emphasize. The trees in the center of the Garden needed to be a pair in order to cross pollinate. Let's go so far as to use God and Satan, as an example of the number two.

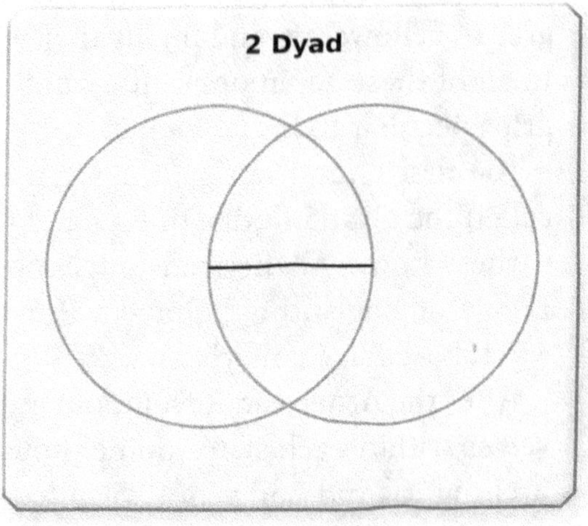

Now to illustrate the number two on a very personal level for you, a neophyte in this Pursuit of Truth Profound: There are two souls in your body right now. One is the celestial, and the other is terrestrial.

THREE. Three is the number of God because one plus two equals three. The New Testament gives us the story of the creation of the Triune God. The puppets sitting on the right hand and left hand of God are His voice, not Him. Many biblical passages depict the Savior listening to the earthlings, and the Holy Ghost whispering instructions in the earthling's ear on how to obey the Almighty. The Holy Ghost cannot make any mistakes, for he is listening to the Almighty, whose wisdom he relays to you as your inner voice.

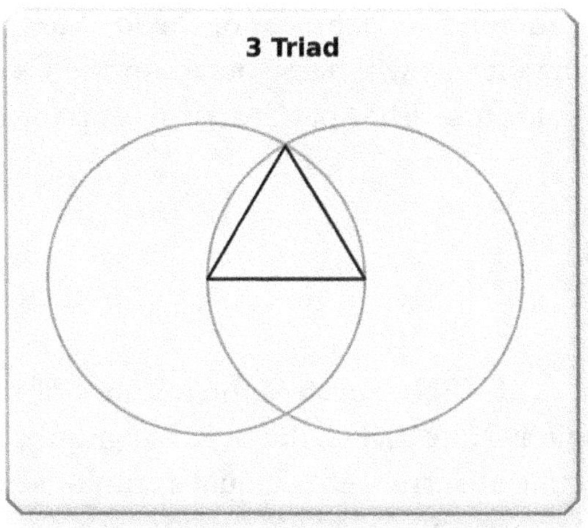

FOUR. Four is the home of God. There were 4 major writing prophets. (Daniel, Ezekiel, Isaiah, and Jeremiah.) There are the 4 horsemen of the apocalypse. There are four points to the Cross of Jesus. (Not all crosses in ancient times had four points. Some were shaped like the capital letter T.) There are four gospels.

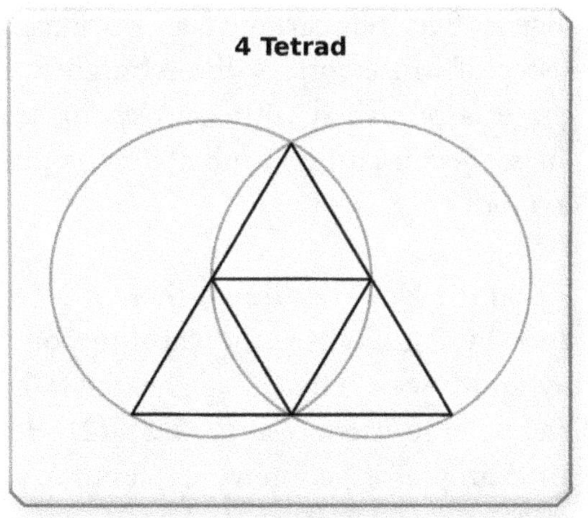

FIVE. Five is the number of regeneration. Slice an apple across the middle, and you will note five sections of seeds. Note that 14 = 1 plus 4 = five. Christ in *Matthew 19:12* mentions eunuchs five times. In *Acts 8:27, 34, 36, 38, & 39* the eunuch is again mentioned five times. (In both cases, the number is five: another example of numerology.)

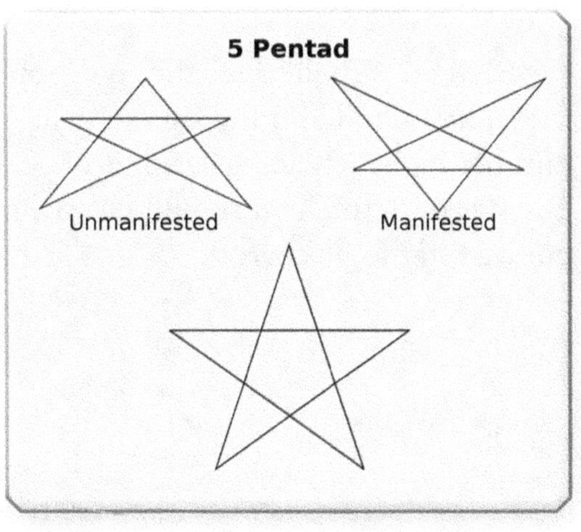

SIX. Six can be seen as the number of The Perfect Man, in harmony with the top triangle of the Triune God and the lower triangle of man with a balanced body, soul and mind. It is the star of David. Meditating on this will help you attain the Celestial Spark. The Spark's arrival is up to you.

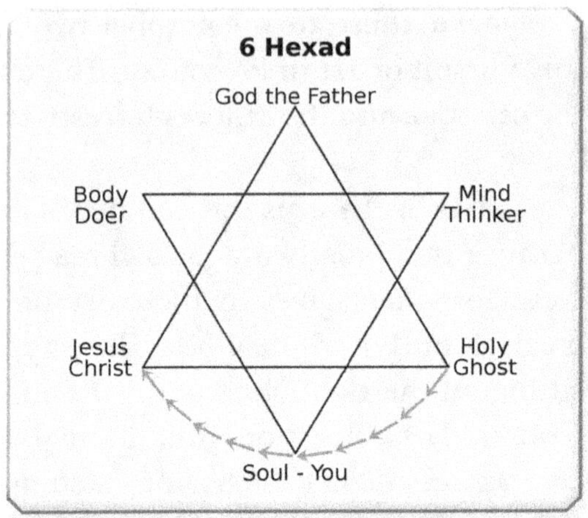

SEVEN. Seven is the number of religion. Note that all the sides of a numbered cube are arranged to equal a sum of seven for opposite sides. (Just look at a pair of dice.) Eve, reincarnated as Miriam, the sister of Moses, upset the Almighty, and she was punished with leprosy for seven days. Seven is the number for the praise to God.

In the New Testament there is a reference by Paul, where the capstone on the pyramid was refused, as he felt Christ had been refused. *(Matthew 21:42)* Here's an example of geometry explaining your spiritual development.

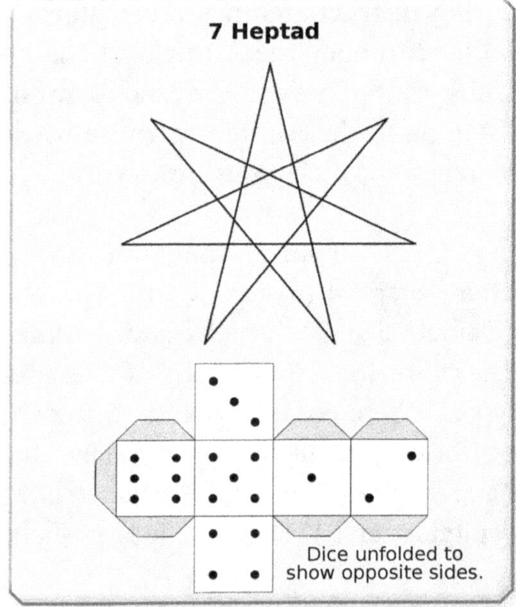

EIGHT. Eight has the position of the sign of good and the sign of evil. The number eight reflects Jesus and or Satan. The star of Bethlehem should be an eight-pointed star to be correct.

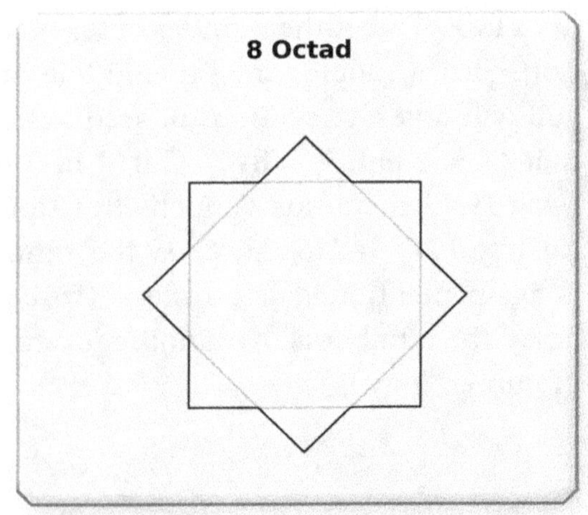

NINE. Nine is the number of the sinner, the imperfect man. It is shaped like sperm. If you multiply any single digit by nine, the two digits in the answer will always add up to nine. For example, 9 X 7 = 63. 6 + 3 = 9. Thus the answer reduces to a one digit number. In other words, nine contains the forces of all the other numbers.

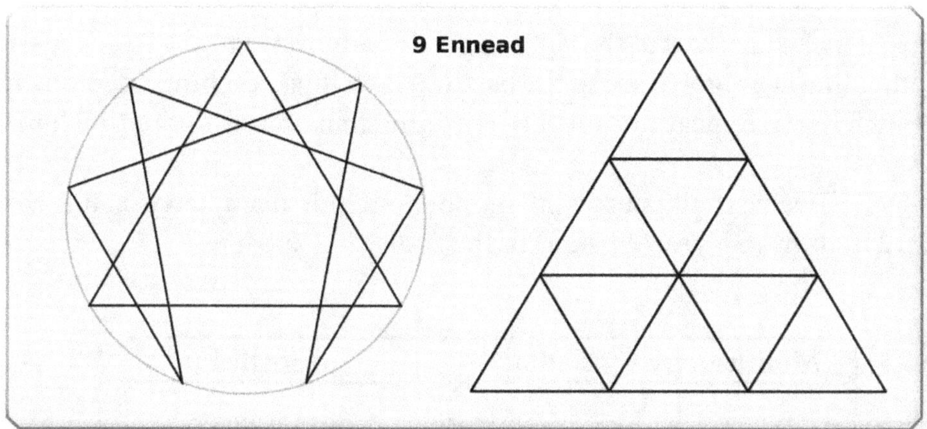

TEN. Ten is the number regarded as the power of God. To raise or lower the number, just move the decimal. There are 10 commandments; 1/10 of your income is a tithe; the were 10 plagues on Egypt; 10 x 10 silver sockets formed the foundation of the Tabernacle.

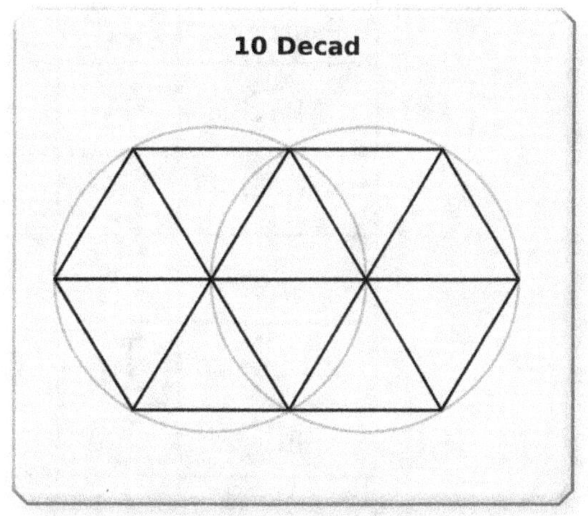

ELEVEN. Eleven has great relevance. It is not always reduced to a one digit number. The square to round triangle has a 10 inch side length and an 11 inch hypotenuse (diameter of the circle).

The ancient laborers used a special ruler to make it easy for the them to exchange a square container for a cylindrical container of the same volume. To construct a ruler for measuring the circle diameter (an 11 inch ruler marked in 10ths) start with a 10 inch line (the size of the square) and then from the right end of

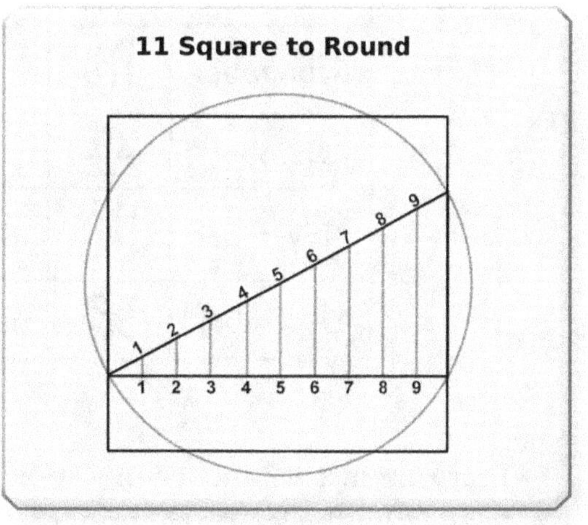

that line draw a line upwards at a right angle. From the left end of the 10 inch line, measure 11 inches towards the vertical line and mark where they cross at 11 inches to form the right angle triangle. That will create a triangle with one side of 10 inches, the hypotenuse of 11 inches and the opposite side of a little over 4 inches.

On the 10 inch side, start at the right angle side and move to the 9 inch mark and make another line at a right angle to the base (10 inch line) reaching up to the hypotenuse (11 inch line). Repeat this for the remaining inch marks to the 1 inch mark.

TWELVE. Twelve is, of course, the number of God: one plus two. It is a magic number: 12 months in a year, 12 signs of the zodiac, 12 apostles.

Months	Zodiac		Apostles
January	♑	Capricorn	Simon Peter
February	♒	Aquarius	James
March	♓	Pisces	John
April	♈	Aries	Andrew
May	♉	Taurus	Philip
June	♊	Gemini	Thomas
July	♋	Cancer	Bartholomew
August	♌	Leo	Matthew
September	♍	Virgo	James
October	♎	Libra	Simon
November	♏	Scorpio	Thaddaeus-Judas
December	♐	Sagittarius	Judas Iscariot

There are also 12 inches in a foot. The width of the average man's thumb was roughly 1/12th the length of the average man's foot.

Twelve is the sum of 3 + 4 + 5 = 12. The 3, 4, 5 triangle is an even sided right triangle. A rope tied into 12 equally spaced knots can be used to make a square corner.

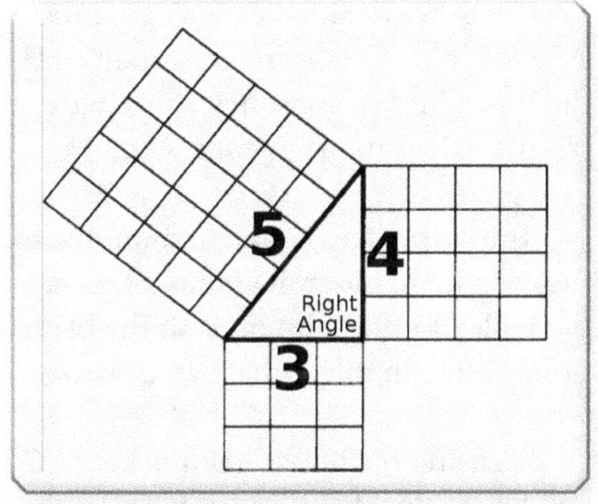

THIRTEEN. Thirteen is the number of the disciples plus the Rabbi Jesus, as well as the number of the original states of America.

FOURTEEN. Fourteen generations is mentioned three times in the Bible. The number of generations from Abraham to David is fourteen, from David to the carrying away to Babylon is fourteen genera-tions, and from Babylon to Jesus, again fourteen generations. *(Matthew 1:17)*

TWENTY-TWO. Twenty-two is another influential number. It can reduce to four, but mostly is kept as twenty two. In numerological analysis, if the month, day, and year of your birth totals either eleven or twenty-two, they are left alone.

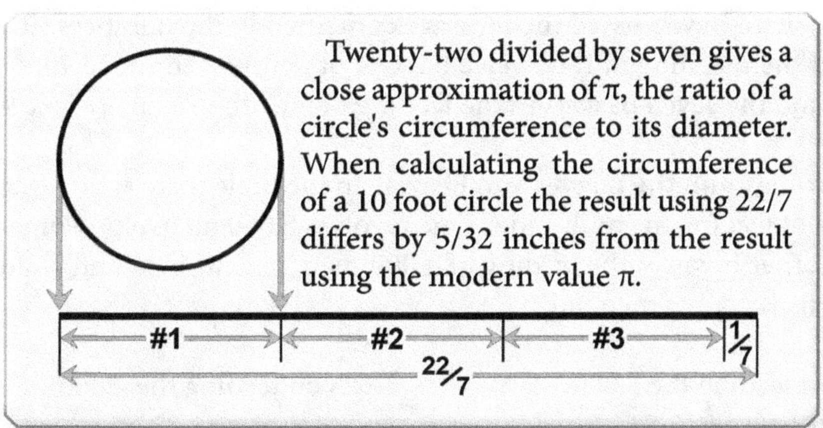

FORTY. The number forty is an appeal for help and signifies a time of testing. Moses was on Mount Sinai for 40 days and 40 nights. The prophet Elijah went 40 days without food or water on Mount Horeb. The children of Israel wandered in the desert for 40 years.

Another example of numerology in the Old Testament is found in the story of Elijah's healing of the widow's son. Elijah had stretched himself on the body of the son three times, and the boy sneezed seven times. Three is the number of God, and seven is the number to praise and glorify the Almighty

Christ was trained in as a carpenter. That meant that he was also trained in mathematics. Numbers were important to Him, and they are important in understanding the Bible. In Freemasonry, the square, already in use in ancient times is a symbol of truth, justice, and righteousness.

The carpenter's square is a unique tool, one that a carpenter will use every day in the exercise of his craft. It has all the math in the universe on the blade. For example, the table of rafter numbers on the blade gives a carpenter a way to do quick calculations based on the Pythagorean theorem.

Perusing the book *"Arithmetic for Carpenters and Builders"* by Jameson and Dale will be invaluable in understanding the significance of numerology, not to mention the fact that the information on the blade of the two-foot carpenters square can help you build a house, lay a foundation, or create a piece of art. (The book, originally published in 1915, has been digitized and is available at no charge on Google Books.)

Christ then, was involved in numbers, and numbers came to have significance beyond his carpentry trade. For example, there is a significance in the numbers associated with the stories of the loaves and fishes. He even remarks to the disciples that they seem to have missed the message contained in the numbers. They did not understand the meaning of the twelve baskets of leftovers in the feeding of the five thousand, and the seven baskets in the feeding of four thousand. *(Mark 8:16–22)*

Numerology and the Loaves and Fishes. In the Bible there are two stories about the miracle of feeding the multitude. One involves 5,000 men, plus women and children. The other involves the feeding of 4,000 men, plus women and children. Note that this census counts men only.

Texts on feeding the 5,000:
Matthew 14:15-21
Mark 6:35-44
Luke 9:12-17
John 6:5-14

Texts on feeding the 4,000:
Matthew 15:32-39
Mark 8:1-9

In the feeding of the 5,000 there were only five loaves of bread. Five is an important number here because it is the number of regeneration. The disciples picked up twelve bushels of leftovers. Note that the five plus two equal seven, the number related to religion. The number twelve is important in the Bible because it is the number of the tribes of Israel, the number of the disciples, the number of months, and the number of signs in the zodiac.

In the feeding of the 4,000 there were only seven loaves and a few small fishes. The number of loaves available was again seven. This time there was no indication as to regeneration, so they picked up seven baskets of leftovers.

Both feedings are discussed in *Mark 8:17-21*. The Rabbi Jesus asked the disciples why they did not understand. Jesus must have hoped for a better understanding of the numbers in the two events. The miracles that the Christ performs have considerable meaning. Grasping the implications of the numbers will further your understanding of the Bible.

Here again is a diagram of The Perfect Man. It is the Star of King David, composed of two triangles. One triangle is the Almighty and his Consorts. The other is you and your consorts. It is important that you accept here and now that the Almighty's triangle is pure, and the triangle of you, the soul, is relegated to dwell in an earthly body.

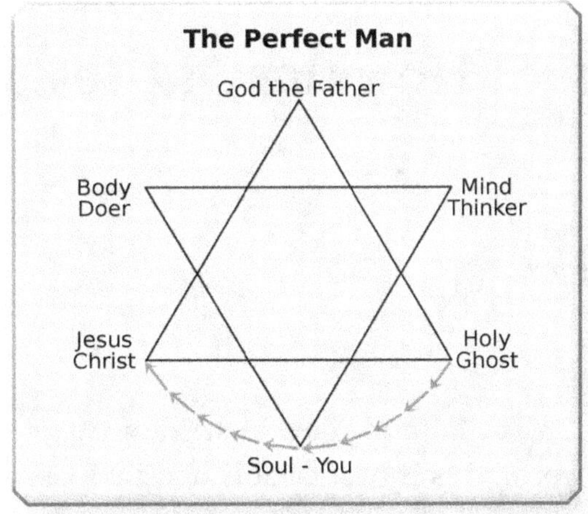

The top triangle is, of course, the Triune Godhead.

The next triangle is the terrestrial, striving to enhance the body and mind of the terrestrial soul to follow the instructions from the Most High.

There are two souls in your body right now. One is the celestial, and the other is terrestrial. How, as a neophyte, do you combine the two souls? The graphic of the number six and the star of David explains to you how this is set up. The Celestial Spark's arrival is up to you. As you listen to the voice within, you will know in your heart what is the correct thing to do. I supposed I should say that you will know in your liver what to do. The liver is the cleanser of bodily toxins and is also important in clearing the way for hearing the voice within.

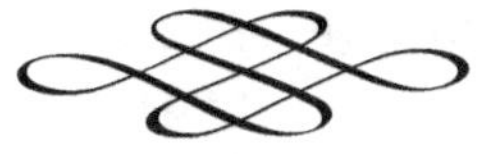

Chapter 5
Reincarnation,
How the Old Testament Writes the New

The author takes in stride that reincarnation is part and particle of the written word. This is best established in *1 Corinthians*. My comments on reincarnation are intended to show how the celestial soul gets into the earthly body.

Constructing this concordance has been very interesting. The authors have taken the characters from one part of the scriptures and then shifted their roles in another part later on.

If you read widely, you will find much of relevance in other sources that will cast light on reincarnation, omophagia, celibacy, and the third eye. Greek mythology has many examples of omophagia by heroes like Achilles, Ajax, and Hercules who felt that consuming the blood and flesh of their defeated adversaries would enhance their own strength. In Geraldine Pinch's book on Egyptian mythology (see Bibliography), you will find fascinating information about the Third Eye and the battle between Set and Horus.

The odd part of the story is that the Hebrew faith does not believe the Messiah had arrived in the time of Herod the Great. This narrative is not devoted to answering that question; we are here to make a case for reincarnation and how it plays an important role in the Biblical story.

In the beginning, when God was not real busy, He went KAZAM! And He had an Angel, the most beautiful of all Angels. This Angel desired God's throne, but the Almighty said, "No! I the Lord thy God, am a jealous God!" And the Angel was cut down. God created the earth, to which He banished the pretender to His throne. The banished angel had a new name, The Evil One. Surprisingly enough, the Evil One was able to garner of third of the host of heaven. But this earth thing was not fit for man nor beast to live on, so the Almighty needed a gardener.

KAZAM! We have the gardener. Formed by the soil from the four corners of this earth we have God's new creation, Adam. Notice that the two KAZAMs created two individuals. Therefore, having the same Creator, Adam and Lucifer are brothers.

The murder of Abel by Cain is a harsh event, as now there is now no way to carry on the existence of Adam's humankind. Consequently, Adam and Eve produce Seth to carry on the lineage.

This repetitive narrative is to establish that the four important individuals in the Old Testament will also be in the New Testament. The Old Testament, using prophecy, wrote the New Testament. Are these same actors to be the actors in the New Testament? Does God desire for Adam to be remembered as the brother to the Evil One?

The final picture has been developed. God has for His two helpers the original characters from the Garden of Eden story, Adam and Abel. They have progressed through the Bible, in form becoming equal. They are both from the seed of the Holy Ghost, God Himself. The female bloodline is just as important; both are of the lineage of Levi. The story is as remarkable and as fascinating as a story could be, beginning in the Garden as a Father, son, and Grandfather triangle, and finishing as the two Sons of the Almighty, each now part of the Triune Godhead. Happy daze, (pun intended), good luck, and God bless. Amen

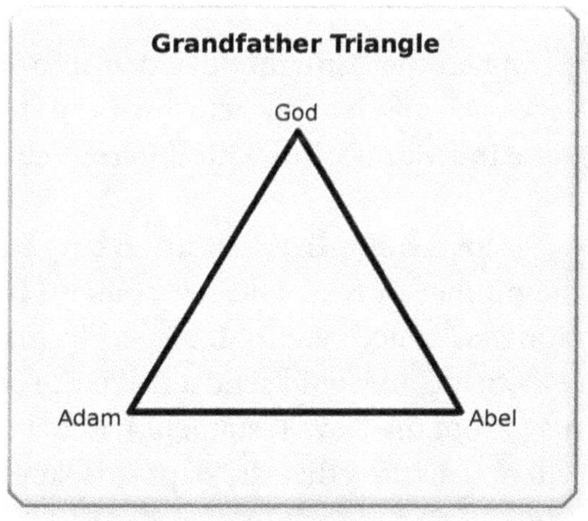

In the beginning, we alluded to bringing the initial actors in the Garden into the new story in the New Testament. It is not too difficult, for the main character, Christ, is Adam reincarnated.

In studying the mother of Christ, it is evident that she was Eve, and possibly Miriam, the sister of Moses and Aaron. This may be speculation, but two examples provide some substantial evidence. At the cross, the mother of Him is with her sister Mary, and there are very few mentions anywhere of two siblings bearing the same first name. The second is that in Aramaic the name for the mother of Him is Mariam, the same as the sister of Moses.

The most important idea here is that the process of passing through the birth canal is very important. Without passing through the canal, it is very unlikely that you will readily be considered human. Adam and Eve produced humans; this was accomplished with the help of the Almighty through two created bodies.

That may seem unimportant, but it is relevant in discussions of cloning in the world today. One of the questions is how will a soul be selected for this new body of dust and clay created by cloning? The idea is that at conception the minds of the two participants are drawing a soul from the soul depository during fecundation.

Adam and Eve were given souls at the time of their creation. This information is important, as Adam was here at the time the Creator laid the foundations of the universe. All the souls there are, are here and now. Solomon said that there is nothing new under the sun. There are as many and maybe more souls than the stars in the sky or the grains of sand on the beach.

When the Almighty decided to bring the promised Messiah to the Jews, it was necessary to select the actors for the story. This treatise will imply that these are the same individuals, but with different names.

John the Baptist. Let us take up first John the Baptist. It is recorded that when the mother of Him told her cousin Elisabeth, The Baptist's mother, that the Son of God was conceived, John leaped in his mothers' womb at the promise made to the Jews that God would send a Leader to conquer the world. This passage indicates that his part of the New Testament had been laid out in heaven by the Heavenly Father. I will make a case that the Baptist is Abel reincarnated.

It will not require too much to imagine that the Father will be selecting Eve as the mother of the Savior. Cain lives here on earth, and all that is needed is the correct character for the role. It will be Herod, the king of Israel.

God did not take just any waif from the streets for the mother of Him. The young girl Mariam was held in high esteem around the synagogue.

There are now three of the actors on stage for Act Two. Mariam is carrying Adam to fulfill the promise of a Savior. *(1 Corinthians 15:45)* John the Baptist has a great role in this act, as the prophet foretelling the coming of the Messiah.

The roles are filled. Eve will be the Mother of Him; Abel will be John the Baptist, and Adam will be Christ. *(2 Corinthians 15:45)*

Abel, as Elisha, received power from Elijah (Elias). John the Baptist received power from Elias (Elijah). *(Matthew 17:11–13)* Fulfilling the prophecy of Jesus being born in Bethlehem, his supposed father was of the lineage of King David.

Notice that in *Matthew 11:8-14,* Jesus identifies John the Baptist with Elias. *In Matthew 17:11-13,* Jesus again identifies John the Baptist with Elias.

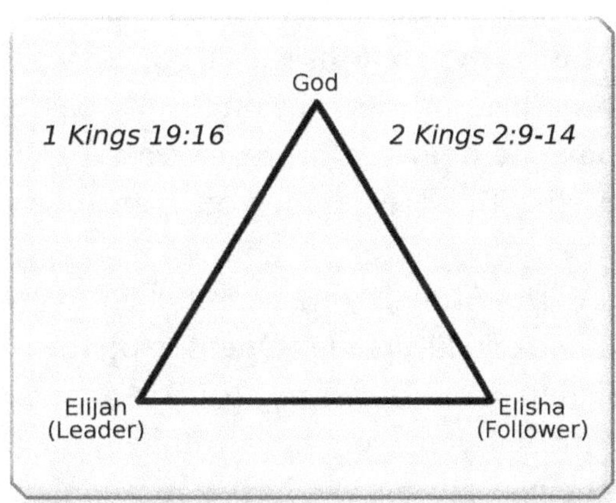

The Baptist had a hairy coat and leather girdle. *(Matthew 3,4,* and *Mark 1:6.)* Elijah was similarly attired. *(2 Kings 1:8)* Elijah dropped his hairy coat to Elisha, and this gave Elisha the powers of Elijah. This establishes the combining of the two stories. Christ at that time was Elijah, and The Baptist was Elisha. In the New Testament, The Baptist is Elijah/Elias *(Matthew 17:10 – 13)* and Christ is Elisha. Elijah anoints Elisha to be his replacement, and in the New Testament, John the Baptist baptizes (anoints) Christ to be his replacement.

This group of passages was difficult for me, as in my thinking they had just exchanged cloaks, but John is actually taking the role of Elijah, not just the cloak, to become the leader in the New Testament. John assumed this role for nearly ten years, until the time of the threes came into the story: three years preaching and Jesus bearing the cross at age thirty three. John then baptized (anointed) Jesus as his successor. As in the Old Testament, *1 Kings 19:16,* this was done in order to ensure Adam and Abel equality in all of life. As part of the Triune Godhead, they are equal in power and strength. And, they are father and son.

The Terrible Twos

The challenge in reading the Bible is that the reader is presented with choices. I call them the terrible twos. There are two souls, there are two paths, there are two leaders, and it is always difficult to know which one to follow. Realizing that there are two will help considerably. The word *Lord* is used in the Bible 7,838 times. The *Lord* that we are concerned with is the *Lord* that embodies the voice within. In Psalm 25, the word is used in two ways, and you must learn which one refers to the voice within.

Adam's Reincarnation. Adam is here in several reincarnations, the purpose being to prepare Him for his eventual role as the Savior of the World. One basis for this reincarnation idea is that there were never any remains found for Adam or Moses. Where Moses was buried was not noted. The Almighty had Elijah end his time here on earth dramatically, taking him to heaven in a whirlwind. Again, we have no bones from the deceased. What's important is that no bones were left on earth. That is explained on Transfiguration Day.

The Almighty was compelled to create Adam. The Father had been entirely too harsh on His people. Opening up the earth and consuming 10,000 of His souls? That had to stop. *(Numbers 16:32)* Adam is slated to be the only Begotten Son. When the time has come and been fulfilled, the Son will assume a pivotal role in ruling earth. The new regime will have a more tolerant and compassionate Leader.

To better understand the Father's plan, notice that there is learning and work being carried on all the time, stretching all the way back to Eden with Eve receiving an education from the actions of Satan. Rules are made to be broken. They must be, they will be, broken and then all is fulfilled. Someone planted those trees in the midst of the Garden for a good reason. Evidence of Adam's being a human began in the Garden. He says, "It's not my sin God, it was that woman, the one *you* gave me."

Adam as Moses. Adam goes through an apprenticeship for his eventual role as the Savior. The first stop is in the body of Moses. This is a very stiff assignment, and Moses does not perform all that well in obeying God's commands. For example, in the story of the water spring Moses strikes the rock, but God had told him only to speak to the rock to show the power – to use mental power, not physical power.

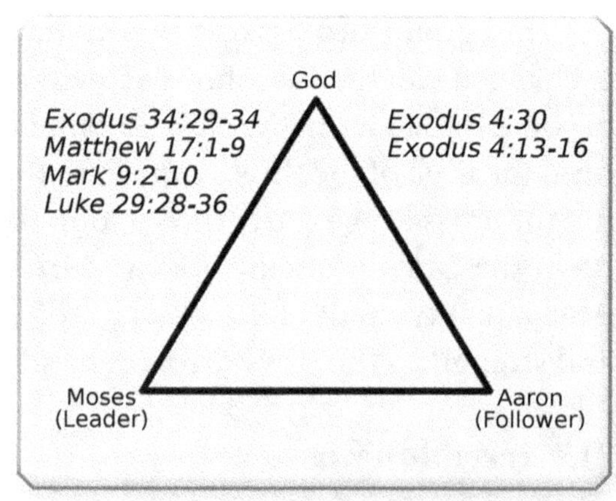

Moses was to be the leader of the Israelites, but he had his failures from time to time during his travels in the desert. God told Moses to hide in the cleft of the rock, so that when God passed by, He could put up His hand so that Moses would not see His face. This act got a lot of mileage, because afterwards Moses had to wear a veil until the blinding glory of God wore off his face. We take this scene as foretelling the return of Moses as the Christ.

In the end, Moses did see the promised land, but he was not allowed to enter it. It is not revealed where Moses was buried. In this Biblical narrative, Moses' sister Miriam is Eve, reincarnated.

Adam as Elijah. The next reincarnation of Adam, the next step in his apprenticeship, is as Elijah, the prophet and predictor of the future. Again the earth yielded no bones. Elijah was taken up from earth in a whirlwind. Adam's reincarnation as Christ is getting closer.

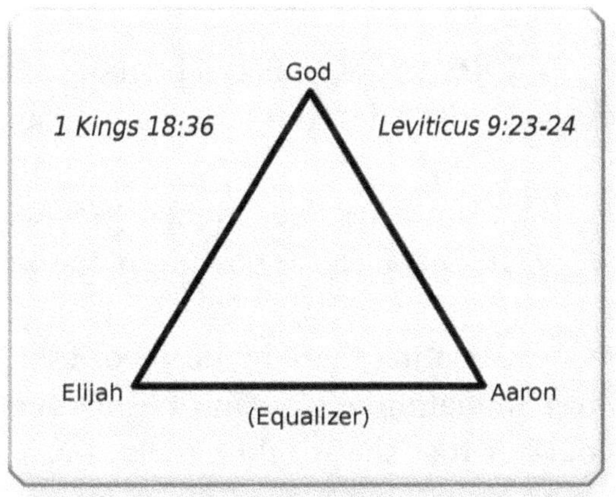

Lineage of Christ. King David had six wives. Which one was the producer of the lineage for the mother of Him? Is it that important that we know? Adam is *a priori*[1] the root of the lineage. So we will dwell on the passages that subscribe to the Christ being Adam in the Garden.

1 Corinthians 15:45 "And so it is written, The first man Adam was made a living soul; the last Adam was made a quickening spirit."

Luke 3:38 "Which was the son of Enos, which was the son of Seth, which was the son of Adam, which was the son of God."

Romans 5:14 "Nevertheless death reigned from Adam to Moses, even over them that had not sinned after the similitude of Adam's transgression, who is the figure of him that was to come."

---

1   Latin: Proceeding from a known or assumed cause to a necessarily related effect; deductive.

Biblical Parallels

- Adam in the Old Testament, with Abel the shepherd *(Genesis 4:4)*.
- John the Baptist in the New Testament with Christ as the shepherd *(John 10)*.

- Elijah with his hairy coat in the Old Testament, with Elisha as his replacement prophet *(2 Kings 1:8,* and *1 Kings 19:16)*.
- The Baptist with his hairy coat *(Matthew 3:4)* and Christ as replacement preacher.

- Adam loses his son in the Old Testament when Cain murders Abel.
- Christ loses his cousin in New Testament when Herod beheads John the Baptist.

- Christ rides to Bethlehem on an ass.
- Christ rides into Jerusalem on an ass.

- Adam takes Eve's hymen *(Genesis 4:1)*.
- This parallels the opening of the birth canal of Mariam (Eve) for the birth of Christ.

Correlating these biblical stories is interesting. Elisha in *2 Kings 4* was taken in by a Shunammite woman. Elisha's servant told him the woman was barren. Elisha told her that she would have a son. This correlates with The Baptist's mother also being barren and having the Baptist in old age. Did the scribes tell us a good story ? The character of John the Baptist is foretold in the Old Testament. He will be the forerunner of the Messiah. *(Isaiah 40:3)*

I take these similarities as part of the development of the New Testament story. The Old Testament prophesied and wrote the New Testament.

We have in the Garden one bad neighbor, Satan, who is able to beguile the lady next door. Eve tells the Almighty that the neighbor deceived her. *(Genesis 3:14* and *1 Timothy 2:14* describe their punishment.) *1 John 3:12* says that Cain was "of the wicked one," i.e. of Satan, not of Adam.

Act Two takes us to the New Testament, in which the angel Gabriel tells the virgin that she will soon bring forth the promised Messiah. *(Luke 1:35, Matthew 1:18,* and *Isaiah 7:14)*

In another parallel, we have the Satan in one sex incident and the Almighty in the other sex incident, thus fulfilling the *two* required acts.

In an interesting aside, the Virgin began as a virgin; after her initial act of sin she was a sinner. In the story of the sister of Moses harassing her older brother, she offended the Almighty, and He punished her with leprosy for seven days. Seven is an important number here.

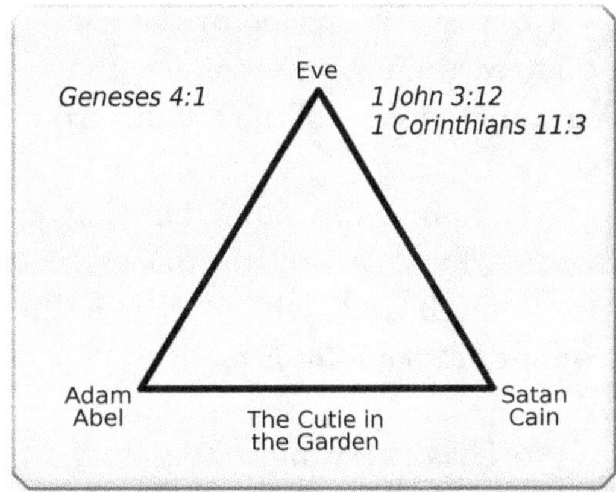

It is relevant that the Virgin had gone through the birth canal, something that Eve had not done. That the name of the mother of Him is Mariam is supported in the Book of Luke. In The Interlinear Bible the entire book of Luke refers to the Virgin as Miriam. This was in the lineage of the priests. To sum up, Eve has as great a role as the Virgin, as Adam does in his dual role of Adam and the Christ.

This TWO thing can get carried away. We have Jesus and John the Baptist, as the two in opposition to the Anti-Christ and the false prophet.

More Bible Correlations. To correlate this mythical documentary with other portions of this tome, follow this:

Adam is the handmade creation of a clay puppet that God brought to life.

As a special creation of God's hand, Adam had to do the work of Moses. The job of savior was initiated for the future. God also made Moses' face shine, as Christ was to shine later.

Adam was Elijah for further instructions in the future.

Adam was given the job as the Savior of the World, to die on the cross and ascend into heaven. To close this part of the great story, we will go directly to Transfiguration Day. On that day we have Moses, Elijah and Christ together as one, for they are one, all Adam's celestial soul. *The number three is now visible.*

At the transfiguration, He was joined by Moses and Elijah. Jesus asked the Father to take the cup from Him. Moses and Elijah came to remind Him that He needed to go on to Jerusalem to fulfill the scriptures. *(Mark 9:4 and Luke 9:30-31)*

Eve was also created by the hand of the Almighty. She had no original connection to earthlings. In keeping with the rules, Eve was Miriam, the sister of Moses and Aaron in the story of the Exodus from Egypt. In this role she was a prophet.

As a young girl around the synagogue, Mariam, the Virgin-to-be, was given much freedom, for she was of the lineage of Aaron. This was all part of the story and necessary to fulfill God's will. As was written, she was to be venerated for all generations to come. *(Luke 1:46-49)*

Abel has a very interesting role. As John the Baptist he was again killed. As John, he never married. He had the role of Elisha along the way, with Adam as Elijah.

The last player of this group needs no introduction, needs no lives in between to lift His education in these matters. He is the best there is. Finds people to do the job all the time.

This collection of evidence from the Bible is to establish that the characters from the Garden of Eden scene appear from time to time in the narratives throughout the Bible, in both the Old and New Testaments. As the image of Elijah is Adam reincarnated, it is only reasonable for Elisha to be Abel - never married and never a wine drinker. The similarities and correlations in this book of books are quite intriguing.

Some further examples:

- Abel is the shepherd in the Book of Genesis, and Adam as Christ is the shepherd in the New Testament. *(John 10)*

- Elijah girdles his hairy coat in *2 Kings 1:8* and The Baptist girdles his hairy coat in *Matthew 3:4* and *Mark 1:6.*

- Elijah anoints Elisha to be his replacement in *1 Kings 19:16,* and The Baptist baptizes Christ to be his replacement in *Mark 1:9.*

- Before delving into this further, the reader must see that the roles are intermittently exchanged. The anointed is selecting the successor.

- Possibly more difficult to grasp now is the concept of Adam and Abel as Elijah and Elisha and finally, as Christ and John the Baptist.

- As Elijah was selecting Elisha in *2 Kings,* Elisha wanted to go home and kiss his mother and father. Elijah (Christ) allowed this to take place. In the New Testament, however, those who desired to go home first, and *then* follow Christ, were denied the request.

Another bit of critical information must be weighed in this pursuit of the truth. In *Matthew 11:11,* Christ says that there is no other man born of a woman greater than the Baptist. In this context, Christ is including Himself. There is no loftier praise from anyone or any place that is higher than passage eleven. The Baptist proclaims that he in not worthy to lace Christ's sandals. *Matthew 3* is a full rendition of praise for the Baptist.

There is one more role for Adam. Adam is Moses. Careful reading will show that Adam is in his apprenticeship in these roles. In the development of the water spring, Moses was to talk to the rock. Instead, Moses chose to strike the rock. God was not happy about how Moses handled this assignment.

Eve shares some of the reincarnations. As the sister to Moses, she understands what it is like to save the world. As Mariam, she is to be the mother of the Christ Child. As Miriam, sister of Moses, she upsets the Almighty, and she has leprosy for seven days. Seven is the number for the praise to God. Later, Mariam will have the opportunity to say something to Jesus about his behavior at the Temple in Jerusalem, and again when he begins His ministry.

I *believe,* not think or know, that these passages will support my position. *1 Corinthians 15:45–58* reflects my spirit and flesh resolve. These passages provide me the most benefit: *Luke 3:38, John 8:58,* and *Romans 5:14* - Adam is the son of God.

In *1 Corinthians 15:47* we have the first man, i.e. Adam, from the earth, and the second man, the Lord from heaven. *Luke 3:38* calls Adam the son of God. In *Luke 4:22,* the physical character of Christ is portrayed as the son of Joseph, the supposed father, and the Christ does not refute this image. The demons in the various Biblical narratives proclaim that he is the Christ, and Jesus admonishes these demons not to tell.

Eve, Miriam, and Mariam. The two reincarnations of Eve are Miriam and Mariam. The Virgin Mother (Mary or Mariam) and her cousin Elizabeth, the mother of John the Baptist, are descended from Miriam's brother, Aaron. *(Luke 1: 5)*

The Birth of Jesus. Eve has been the Almighty's love since He created her in the Garden. *Luke 1:35:* "The angel answered and said unto her, The Holy Ghost shall come upon thee, and the power of the Highest shall overshadow thee: therefore also that holy thing which shall be born of thee shall be called the Son of God." *Isaiah 7:14* proclaims that a virgin will conceive.

The Almighty runs around and does as He pleases; you would think He owns the place.

The angel Gabriel appears to Mariam and proclaims that she has great favor in the eyes of the Lord. The Almighty has selected her to be the mother of His Child. She is to marry a man named Joseph, selected to be the supposed father, as he is a righteous man.

The Almighty must follow His own rules, so the passing over of the Virgin is done by God. There is no way He can relegate the seduction of the Virgin who will give birth to His only Son. But curious questions arise. Just how large of a hole in the hymen would be required for the sperm to pass into the vagina? Is this something that the Maker of the universe could or would do? We do not know how the Devil did his deed in the Garden, but I'm sure the Almighty passed over in missionary mode. He should; it is His game, and He calls the plays.

Soon after the shadow of the Holy Ghost passes over Mariam, she leaves to visit her cousin Elizabeth, who is five months pregnant with John the Baptist. She stays about three months before returning to Nazareth.

Joseph, an older widower is to be her husband. But when he sees the young girl, she appears to be with child. While Joseph is puzzling over what to do, an angel comes to him and tells him to marry the girl.

When it comes time for Joseph to pay his taxes, the couple must travel to Bethlehem. Mariam is great with child and rides on an ass. It's certain that help from others was needed for the journey. The young girl would not have been able to walk that distance when she was that close to delivering a baby.

A midwife named Salome is assisting with the delivery. She has heard that the mother is purported to be a virgin, but she does not believe it. Salome makes an inspection and her hand withers. It is made whole again when she bathes the newborn Child. The supposed father notes this event and takes it to heart. Salome's hand withered due to her doubt. Her hand was renewed as she bathed the little Christ Child. The meaning was clear. This was indeed the Holy Child.

It is important to understand that to comply with the laws of nature, Eve had to adhere to the ways of nature and become human. Going through the birth canal made her human and she became Miriam. The mother of Mariam was told, "The daughter you will have is destined to do a great service. The daughter will be the mother of the Messiah."

This story comes from an article written about that period that appeared in BAR (*The Biblical Archaeology Review*). The name Mariam appears in the Book of Luke referencing the mother of the Messiah. In the narratives concerning the identity of those at the cross, there is a passage mentioning the sister of the mother of the Christ at the cross, and her name is Mary. The question is, did their parents give the same first name to two girls? Luke, along with me, does not think so. (From *The Interlinear Bible, Luke 1:34*, page 786.)

Abel as John the Baptist. The part of the character Abel in the story is interesting. Abel was slain by his brother Cain. No later stories had an immediate place for the young man. But God had a job for Abel all the time, reincarnated as John the Baptist, the son of Zacharias. The angel appeared to Zacharias, a temple priest, and informed him that his wife Elisabeth would bear a son. His name was to be John. In the past, John had been Abel, the son of Adam; this time he would be the cousin of Adam.

Adam has arrived at the Messiah job the Father in Heaven had planned. Abel, as John the Baptist, would preach and teach for about ten years before the Son Of God was to make an appearance. John had come with good credentials, the best lineage. He took no alcohol and subsisted on honey and locusts during his teaching in the desert. Not all followers of John the Baptist followed Christ. After Christ was baptized, the time left for John on this earth was very short.

Jesus Begins His Ministry. Jesus moves to Capernaum on the Sea of Galilee, where he begins his ministry. His first obligation is to be baptized. When He goes to the Jordan, John the Baptist recognizes Jesus and baptizes Him. The dove comes down, and a voice from above proclaims, "This is My Beloved Son."

The following day, Jesus returns and John's follower, Andrew, decides to follow Jesus. Andrew proclaims to his brother Simon Peter that he has found the Messiah. The next day Jesus meets Phillip and summons him also to follow. Phillip tells his friend Nathanael that he has found the Messiah. Nathanael retorts, "Can anything good come from Nazareth?" Phillip answers, "Come and see."

The words of Jesus are very important when He proclaims that Abel never defiled his body, not at the Garden time, nor at the time of being the forerunner of the Messiah. This role as a metaphorical eunuch is very on point with the idea of staying celibate.

The life of the Baptist is a little sad, for he is destined to be put to death in Act Two, just as he was as Abel in Act One. Just what is the reward for being willing to be done in, in both episodes? Well, Abel had no choice; the Boss makes the rules.

To sum up, we have Adam as the Christ, Eve as the Virgin Mother, Abel as the Baptist, and finally Cain as Herod the Great. Everyone has a role in the first act and in the final act. There are many angles here: Christ and the prophet, then the Anti-Christ and False Prophet, the good and the evil.

The first story ended with four characters, Adam and Eve, Cain and Abel. In the second story, there are only two characters at the cross. This makes for an interesting ending. The two that started from nothing ended up in heaven and are then as nothing here on earth. This could be incorrect, but it's a thought, a possibility. Jesus was to hang on the cross as a criminal, and Eve was to appear as the mother of a criminal. The two syndrome looms up again. The two were saints in the Garden, on both sides of the good and evil fence, in a Hegelian dialectical conflict.

The True Story on the Glory of God

There are several paths of investigation for the seeker of knowledge to grasp the size and magnitude of the powerful God. This is an effort to bring forth the full glory of the Almighty and what He does in an effort to show Himself to the world.

The picture of Satan is complex. In some circles he is considered an angel. But Satan impregnated Eve. *1 John 3:11-14* provides evidence that Satan was more than an angel. Angels are not able to impregnate women. He is referred to as a snake that crawls on the ground; his punishment for his this contribution to Eve is that when he moves about now, he must crawl. Very humiliating. In contrast, in *John 3:14* the serpent is held in high esteem as the healer of snakebites to the Israelites and later is venerated with Christ. Satan misused the serpent for his advantage.

We know from the story in the Garden that it was Eve who was the first to be involved in sin. God was not really very angry with Eve; He only gave her suffering in child bearing as punishment. Eve was the concubine of Satan in the Garden, and as it is in all of sin, there needs to be another act of no sin, an expiation, to bring out the balance of nature. (Sex itself is not a sin. Having children is not a sin.)

The Almighty impregnates the mother of Christ. *(Luke 1:35, Matthew 1:20)* Like Satan in the Garden, the Almighty as the Holy Ghost does not disturb the hymen. Now we have Eve as God's concubine. We have nature in balance: Eve once out of favor, but now in the favor of the Almighty. The terrible twos again, good and evil. To aspire to the born again status, Mariam must now remain chaste, celibate, and be in the favor of the Almighty.

Did the story of the Tree in the center of the Garden of Eden and the eventual eating of the fruit have a bearing on the development of Adam to become Christ and save the world? God used His power to create Satan and Adam. Since the Creator made both creatures, they are brothers. This brotherhood will need to be sundered, and that takes place in the New Testament.

God created Adam for this eventual event, and His Power was in His Word, that He made flesh, with the important mission of entering this realm of earth. The son of perdition rules earth, and Adam is on a par with Satan.

It is written that overpowering Satan required a human, a man, not a God. In this part of the story, Jesus had the soul of Adam, and the Power of the Almighty was ready and available for Jesus to call on and use, as Jesus deemed necessary. In *Hebrews 2:7*, Christ is born of the Virgin, lower than the Angels.

This is a good time to recall the story of the woman who was healed by touching the robe of Jesus. Christ did not know her and did not choose to heal her. The Father did it without the permission of His Son. God does not need Jesus. *We* need Jesus. The Almighty put Jesus here to seek and to save the ones who are lost, the followers of Satan. You are one of the chosen, and it is paramount that you continue to follow God's wishes and increase the light of your soul.

Studying the lives of Christ and The Baptist reveals that their lives were entwined for many moons. These passages liken The Baptist to Elias (Elijah). *John 12:36-43* and *Matthew 17:11-13*. "And Jesus answered and said unto them, Elias truly shall first come, and restore all things. But I say unto you, That Elias is come already, and they knew him not, but have done unto him whatsoever they listed. Likewise shall also the Son of man suffer of them. Then the disciples understood that he spake unto them of John the Baptist." This writer finds the reincarnation useful in describing the connection.

The entire collection of these related stories illustrates the educational plan God implemented for His principle players in order for them to realize their roles of becoming a part of the Triune God: Savior and Redeemer for Christ, and Comforter and Voice within for The Baptist.

Creation of the Triune is what the Bible is about. We return to the investigation here with *Luke 1:5–24 & 41.* Elisabeth is filled with the Holy Ghost, as her cousin The Virgin mother of Christ was filled with the Holy Ghost in *Matthew 1:18.* The reader must come to understand that this spirit that fills both women is not the Comforter Christ promises to the disciples; it is God the Holy Ghost. There is no Triune God in this scene.

The creation of the Triune is what the Bible is all about. God was searching for someone to do the work. Since no one came to His rescue, He created this plan initiated from the day he created Adam, Eve and Abel. Satan was already a work in progress at the Garden of Eden. Satan introduced Cain to the mix.

The cousin Elisabeth had to be brought into the story at some time It well could have been she was one of the women in the narrative of Elijah and Elisha. Elisabeth is important in the New Testament. After years of being barren, there was celestial help for her to become pregnant and filled with the Holy Ghost. God had to be in charge of His plan. God cannot violate His own rules. Christ is His only begotten Son, and The Baptist is His personal replacement. God made the rules for Moses, but this new Holy Ghost is your constant companion, willing to help you all the time, all you have to do is listen.

In all of ol' Bill's efforts in leading you around by your big ears, the Triune God is like this: God sits on the top, His Son sits on a throne to His right hand, and at the other side of the triune head is John the Baptist as the Holy Ghost. AMEN

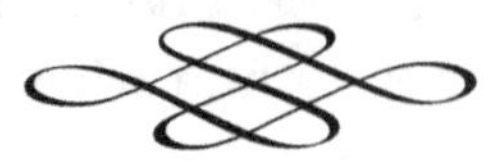

Chapter 6
Ears & Reincarnation

This next aspect of gaining the Celestial Spark relates the shape and size of your ears to the number of times you have been reincarnated. This is most intriguing and may appear to be more full of malarkey than anything else presented in this book. You've read in the book of Matthew, "He who has ears to hear, let him hear." Well, this is entirely different. The size and shape of the ear is the secret. "Listen," the ears tell ones who know and understand, "Those big ears have been here many times."

Everyone has ears. Some are large and have long lobes with many punches for ornaments. Any adornment to the body is of no consequence to this narrative. That is part of your free will and your participation in any of the "follow the crowd" acts; it is not to be judged. There are some passages in the Bible telling of putting an awl to a person's ear, which brands them as a person's servant. *(Exodus 21:6)* Other references say that women can do as they please with adornments.

Ears have been used by the Hindus, the Tibetans, and the Chinese from time immemorial to analyze an individual and his or her past reincarnations. You may have seen the movie *Unbroken*. Photos of the man on whom the movie is based, Louie Zamperini, show his very large ears.

The very first paragraph of an article in the American Legion magazine of December 1, 2014 tells of a person in Zamperini's audience who raises his hand and informs the crowd that in 1957 he had attended the Victory Boy's camp founded by

Zamperini 1952. It was at Louie's camp that this man had accepted the mantle of Christ and become a Christian.

What is this all about? It is about the exposure to a good person, close to going to heaven, but one who did not pass muster to be born again so as to free him from the big book that St. Peter has with the names written for admittance to heaven. First of all, we have not arrived at that point in time to open that book. The guy with the big ears has been a good guy several times but has somehow not made the change to enter into heaven.

The size and length of the ears indicates how many times a person has been reincarnated here on earth. Look for yourself at some gathering. The people with large ears, men and women, will be the good people in the crowd, people treating their fellow men with honor and dignity. You see them at the fund raisers, the charity drives, and other such events.

The explanation of all of this is simple; they may believe, but they did not follow all of the rules, or get the Celestial Spark. These big ears are listening to the voice within; however, they have little knowledge of the voice of the Spark. That is sad and brings me to the primary reason for writing this tome on *how to get the Spark*. It is the undying effort to wake up as many individuals as possible, and once awakened, to have them take the Spark pledge. Zamperini is an example you should definitely desire to follow. The size of the ears tells me that this path he has just finished he has already trod many times in the past.

Zamperini was no doubt listening to the voice within, but did not arrive at the full understanding that would have generated the desire necessary to qualify for the entrance into heaven. The lesson of the story of the three criminals on the cross with Christ is to accept the Spark and to live the way required of the Spark. That's all. That old free will is as great a helper as it is a nuisance.

After Louie's plane went down, he was able to survive 47 days. He was captured by the Japanese. After the war, there were bouts of drinking and despair. But Billy Graham made an impression on good ol' Louie, and he took on the mantle of the Lord. Louie died July 2, 2014.

Prior to the saving of the ex-GI, Louie suffered enormously. In the POW camp the treatment of the men was deplorable. One Japanese Sergeant was very difficult to understand, and it was hard to avoid his wrath. Such events were also prevalent in Louie's earlier existences.

Why do I assume that Louie had many previous lives? His big ears. After hearing his story, do you think that his name should be in the book for entry into heaven in the end times? The greatness of his handling of his life while in the service, and his return to Japan years later to forgive all his captors for the punishment he endured is amazing. The size of his ears shows that Zamperini had done this many times before, but had never taken the Spark to harbor.

There are 120 entries for *ear* and 151 for *ears* in *Strong's Concordance*. In *Genesis 47:5–27* the ears have a relationship to the number seven. *Ear* appears in *Leviticus 14:14* regarding the seven-day cleansing of a man afflicted with leprosy; the man should return on the eighth day. Eight is the number of good and evil. His name will be in the book when they conduct the reading of who will be admitted to heaven and who will be left in the lake of fire.

The subject of the ear is extremely interesting. The top of a well placed ear should not be below the level of the outside corner of the eye socket. It should have considerable girth. Large and floppy or tight to the side of the skull does not matter. The outside of the ear should have a considerable lobe. The larger the ear and the longer and larger the lobe, the greater the number of times this ear has been around the block.

If you look closely, you will see that in some ears the outside line goes right to the skull, in a rather direct circle. This would indicate a rather young ear. The ears play an important part in the disposition and countenance of the person attached to the particular ear you are watching.

Take a look at your own ears. Hopefully you will have a good lobe for your earrings, with a lobe hole in place.

If you are a member of a Masonic Lodge Hall or a similar organization, take an inventory. The members are both young and old here on earth, but how does their age show up by ear evaluation?

The old guys with the long and big ears will turn out to be pretty nice, with a well-balanced disposition, though they may not necessarily be religious. This aspect of their character has come from their many past lives. This kind of spirit on earth recognizes that the simpler life without a lot of fanfare is easier to live with.

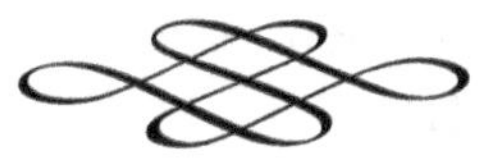

Chapter 7
The Story of Moses

The story of Moses is key to understanding the story of Jesus, as well as to grasping the idea that the Old Testament writes the New Testament.

The Israelites, subjugated by the Egyptians, were cooking, cleaning, making bricks, pulling stone sledges, and doing any other work at hand. They'd been promised something better, and they were unhappy. However, God really did want His people to enjoy the land He had promised them, the land of milk and honey. A leader was needed who would guide the Israelites out of Egypt. God developed a plan.

Things looked grim for the Israelites. Pharaoh had decreed that all the Hebrew boys were to be killed. The Israelites had multiplied, and Pharaoh did not want their population to grow large enough to declare war on the Egyptians.

God had reincarnated Eve as Miriam, the sister of Moses. The mother of Moses had an idea of how to save her son from death at the hand of the Egyptians. She put him in a basket and let it float along the Nile to the spot where Pharaoh's daughter bathed. It was Miriam's chore to watch the babe and report what happened.

When the Princess took the basket out of the water, she saw that it contained a small child. The sister of the babe flew to the Princess's side and enquired if she needed a nurse to care for the young babe. The Princess replied that indeed she did need help. Miriam offered to find someone. Of course, the help conveniently turned out to be Moses' mother herself. The plan of God was working.

The Princess named the babe Moses. Moses grew up and was educated in the King's court. When he was older, he visited the work areas and watched his fellow Hebrews make bricks. One day he witnessed an overseer beating one of the Jews, and in the fray Moses killed the overseer. Thinking that no one had seen what happened, Moses came again the next day. The Jews asked Moses if he would also kill them. It thus became necessary for Moses to leave the country.

Moses met and married a girl named Zipporah, the daughter of Reuel. Zipporah was from what is now Ethiopia and her father was a priest of another faith. God came to Moses and explained His plan to free His people. Moses told God that as a speaker he was not of much value. God instructed Moses to enlist the aid of his brother Aaron. Moses and Aaron went to Pharaoh and asked him to release the Jews. You can imagine the kind of reception they got.

Pharaoh refused. Who would build his monuments and tombs, if not the Jews? Who would clean his palace? Who would cook his meals? Pharaoh's decision was a big mistake because the Egyptians then endured years of terribly unpleasant events: frogs everywhere, and locusts. Their water turned into blood. There were clouds of flies. Painful boils. And finally, all the first-born sons in the land began to die. Except for those of the Jews. Pharaoh now saw the wisdom of setting the Jews free.

Free at last, the Jews were nearing the Promised Land, and Moses sent some scouts ahead to reconnoiter. *(Numbers 13:25)* Forty days later, the scouts came back with terrible news. There were giants in the land, and who wants to go up against giants?

The people's fearful attitude angered the Almighty, and He exiled them to the desert for forty years. By that time all the people who had refused to go into the promised land would be dead. Moses and God's people traveled around the desert for the allotted time.

Moses had a load of work to do. The Jews were not always good. God would be greatly angered, and Moses would have to bear the brunt of the wrath of God. Moses was scorned constantly by the people. God could retaliate severely. In one such trial, God punished 10,000 of the Israelites by opening the ground and swallowing them in the earth.

One of Moses' well-known assignments was to deliver the ten commandments. This gave Moses an opportunity to get close to God. God blessed Moses by making his face shine very brightly, so Moses had to wear a veil over his face when he was with other Jews. This foretold that the Almighty was grooming His Son for the eventual job of being God's cup bearer and saving the people. When they finally were back to the promised land for the second time, Moses was allowed to see the land, but he was not allowed to enter. Where Moses is buried was not recorded for a good reason. *Moses was Adam reincarnated.*

The story of Miriam began at the place where the Princess bathed. We need to emphasize some of the contributions Miriam made to the story during the forty years in the desert. Her brother Aaron was given the title of priest and the task of being one of the holy people whose responsibility it was to care for the tabernacle.

Miriam and Aaron gave Moses a hard time about his foreign family and his father-in-law. Aaron does not fall as far from grace for this transgression as Miriam does. She is punished with leprosy and banished for seven days outside of the camp. Her reincarnation, Mariam of the New Testament, is of the same lineage as Aaron, and that will play a part in her becoming the Mother of Him.

Miriam had no children, but in her reincarnation as the Virgin, she will have a son, and he will be called Jesus.

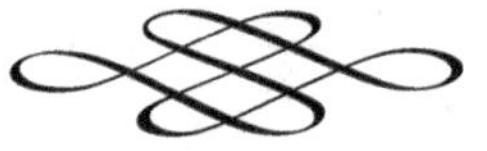

Chapter 8
The Story of Elijah

An important character in this tale is Elijah the Tishbite, an individual with tremendous abilities. First of all, he caused a severe drought. The Almighty then had him go to a small stream where he could drink the water and where the ravens would feed him twice a day. However, this small stream also dried up and the voice within instructed him to go to Zerephath.

A widow in Zerephath was selected to care for the prophet during his stay. Elijah, being hungry, asked the widow to make him a cake. The widow told the prophet that she had only enough for her and her son, and after it was gone they would surely die.

Elijah insisted, and she did as he wanted. The meal in the bowl never ran out, and the oil bottle never ran dry. In a little time, the widow's son became so sick that he died. The widow blamed Elijah; she felt that the death happened because Elijah had moved in with the family. Elijah took the boy to his loft, and three times he was stretched across the boy. The Almighty renewed the boy's spirit, bringing him back to life. The widow then exclaimed that surely Elijah was a man of God.

Moving on, Elijah encountered another man of God, Obadiah, a leading worker for the bad Israelite King Ahab, whose wife was the infamous Phoenician, Jezebel. Elijah asked Obadiah to tell Ahab that he was in town, as the drought was still severe, and he thought Ahab needed to give up the heathen Jezebel's gods so that the rain would come. Obadiah replied that Ahab would surely kill him if he were to go to Ahab with such a story. Finally convinced, Obadiah relayed the message to Ahab, and King Ahab met with Elijah. The subject of their conversation was whose God the Israelites were to praise.

The disagreement would be decided by the outcome of an offering. Two bullocks were brought, one for Ahab's prophets and one for Elijah. Whose deity would be powerful enough to ignite the offering? Ahab's prophets were first, and they could not get the fire to come, even after praying all day and into the evening.

It was Elijah's turn. Elijah prepared an altar with 12 stones representing the sons of Jacob. He then cut up his calf, and placed it on the wood. Elijah dug a moat around the offering that would hold two bushels of seed. Elijah ordered the servants to fill some jugs with water and pour it over the offering and wood. This was done three times. Elijah prayed for the Almighty to light the fire, and the flames consumed the bullock, the wood, and the water. Elijah then had the false prophets slain.

Elijah told his servant to go to the sea and scan the horizon. The servant came back and said he did not see anything. Elijah told him to go seven times. The seventh time the servant saw a dark cloud. Elijah told Ahab that he'd better get home before the rain. When the rain came, it was a real downpour. Jezebel was not happy, as her god Baal had lost the battle. *(1 Kings 18:43)*

Elijah traveled to Jezreel, arriving ahead of Ahab. When Ahab told his wife all that Elijah had done, Jezebel told Elijah that she would kill him, so he skedaddled out of there right fast. *(1 Kings 19:5)* He hid in the woods and fell asleep under a juniper tree. The Angel came and awakened him with something to eat. The Angel came a second time, after which Elijah did not eat again for forty days and forty nights, afterwards going to Mount Horeb and finding rest in a cave.

While he's relaxing and recuperating, The Almighty shows up and gives him his next job. He is to go to Damascus and anoint Hazael as the King of Syria, and after that to anoint Jehu to be King over Israel. When he has accomplished this, he is to seek Elisha and anoint him as his own replacement.

Elijah and Elisha connect and start traveling together. They leave Gilgal and go on to Bethel, where the Ahab's son King Ahaziah has had a fall and is mortally wounded. Ahaziah has sent messengers to ask advice of the idol Baalzebub.

Elijah's instructions were to intercept these messengers and tell them to go back to the king. Ahaziah asks, "Who is this man?" When the messengers describe the man, the king exclaims, "It is Elijah." He sends fifty men and a captain three times to kill Elijah. Big mistake. Elijah calls down the fire of heaven on the first two groups. When the captain of the third group begs for mercy, Elijah grants it because the captain has returned to the God of Israel.

The followers of God tell Elisha that he is about to lose his leader, but he already knows that. Elijah and Elisha head for Jericho near the Jordan River. When they arrive, the sons of prophets there also tell Elisha that the leader is about to die. When the prophet and his disciple arrive at the river bank, Elijah takes off his cloak and smites the water; the two walk across on dry ground to the other side.

Elisha has a last request of Elijah. He desires a double amount of Elijah's spirit. Elisha might be able to claim that gift if he were able to see Elijah as he is taken up to heaven.

Suddenly there comes a fiery chariot and with it a whirlwind, and Elijah is swept up to heaven in the whirlwind. As Elisha watches, the cloak of Elijah falls to Elisha. With the mantle of Elijah, Elisha smites the water and there is dry ground for him to cross the river.

Elisha continues in the path of Elijah in performing miracles and doing good. A widow comes to Elisha and asks for help in saving her two sons. There is a great debt, and the collectors want to take the young men to pay off the debt. Elisha asks the widow, "What do you have in your house?" She says, "We have nothing except some oil in a bottle."

Elisha instructs the widow to venture out and obtain as many empty oil bottles as possible. "Take the bottles home," he tells her, "and behind closed doors, take the bottle of oil that you have and pour oil into the empty bottles." The widow follows his directions. "What should I do next?" she asks, Elisha. Elijah replies, "Why, sell the oil and pay the bills, of course."

Elisha performs many miracles. As Abel reincarnated, it is only reasonably that his work should be prophetic. For example, a Shunammite woman who has prepared a place for him to rest in her home is childless. When Elisha discovers this, he has his servant Gehazi tell the woman to come to the door. As she stands there Elisha tells her that in time she will bear a son. She doubted, like Martha, but she conceives and bears a son.

This son later goes into the fields with his father and has a headache. He is taken to the house and by noon he is dead. The woman goes to her husband, seeking a fast ass, so she can go to the man of God. Elisha sees her coming tells his servant to go to meet her. The Shunammite woman throws herself at the feet of Elisha, and the servant restrains her.

Elisha calls off the servant, and listens to the woman's story. He gives his staff to the servant and instructs Gehazi to put it on the child's forehead. There is no recovery, so Elisha comes to the house himself, and the child is dead.

Elisha enters the room and closes the door. He puts his mouth to the son's mouth, his hands on his hands, and stretches out on the son's body. The flesh is warm. Elisha leaves the room and walks the floor. Time passes and Elisha returns to the son. While he stretches across the boy, the boy sneezes seven times. He is alive! Another miracle and another example of numerology.

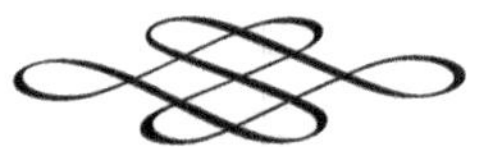

Chapter 9
Jesus is Not God

What motivated me initially to do an in-depth study of the scriptures and other literature was my disagreement with the belief of so many people that Christ is GOD. It's not a problem if you disagree, but I'd like you to hear my arguments. You're young, but I can have my exit at any time.

It is my contention that Jesus is not God. If not, then how does Jesus fit into the picture? Was he wholly human? Was he partly divine? Was he a blend? *John 1:14* is interesting. "The Word was made flesh, and dwelt among us." It does not say that God was made flesh, but that the Words of God were made flesh.

Is Jesus God, or does He have some other position in heaven and earth? I will be using the words of Jesus from the scriptures as a foundation for my views.

The sculptor Pygmalion of Greek myth had the power to make stone come to life. In Genesis, God makes dirt come to life. The soul of Adam, like all other souls, has been here since the big bang. Adam is God's creation and will be His only Son in a later incarnation. *(1 Corinthians 15:45)* The entire mission of the Messiah was planned in detail in heaven.

My intent is to tell mortals that Christ is not God, but God does the work through Christ. What I want you to know is what I believe, that God does not need Jesus. You do.

God needed someone to do the work; it was necessary to have His Son for the job. The entire story of the birth of Christ and the mission of the Messiah, leading into the mission of John the Baptist, was conceived for this purpose, right down to the selecting of Judas to be the one to betray Christ. The story could have been different had Judas accepted Christ; he had the time when he had done the deed. But it was evident that something special on his part was necessary to complete God's plan.

The Back-Story. The angel Gabriel tells a certain young lady that she has been chosen. *(Matthew 1:18, 20, and Luke 1:35)* There is as yet no Triune God; this Holy Ghost is the Almighty Himself, in the form of a Shadow. To authenticate the story we have the Baptist leaping in his mother's womb when he hears that the Messiah is on His way as planned.

The Holy Ghost in this case is God. In the future John the Baptist will become the Holy Ghost, sitting on the left hand of God. Mere mortals do not understand the magnitude of this work of coming to earth. Gods do not get here through the birth canal. That would be undignified, humiliating. But Jesus came here through a birth canal, *and so was born a man.*

When Jesus was about two years old, the Wise Men came to visit the house of the new King and His mother. *(Matthew 2:11)* Herod understood the Wise Men's story of Jesus to mean that there would be an attempt to take his throne, so he ordered all children under the age of two to be killed. *(Matthew 2:16)*

Joseph is referred to as the father, and the neighborhood accepted this as true. God selected Joseph to be the reputed father, because he was a righteous man. But as *Matthew 1:25* states, the marriage was not consummated prior to the birth of Christ. This passage leaves us with an unanswered question. Did Joseph consummate the marriage at all? He was an older man and had not been with a woman for some time, although he had children from a previous family. Did he then take on God's selection for the mother of His only Son to be for his pleasure, concubine, or wife? I don't think so. If you go to Joe's Bar and Grill down on the corner, you will find some of the women there are not for you to horse around with; they are verboten. That may have been the case with Mariam as the Holy Mother, a virgin.

Jesus is like us, as we are like Him. Our soul is the part and particle of the Almighty. So was Jesus Christ. It is important to understand that Christ is no different than you and I are, except that His light is very bright, and the brighter your Soul's light, the heavier the load will be for you to carry during your next learning experience here on earth.

God is a jealous God, unwilling to share his omnipotence with any one - not with Satan, which is proven, nor even with Christ, which Christ is not going to challenge.

Jesus tells us again and again that He and the Almighty are one, but that the Almighty is greater than he is. *(John 14:28).* The relationship is explained in *John 5:26, 27.* God the Father is in himself, and Christ is in himself. The two are individuals, *not* one and the same.

Christ tells of seeing the Father. Well, that would be difficult if they were one and the same, because Christ would be seeing himself. He would need a mirror, wouldn't He? Jesus says that you must come to the Father through Christ, that the Son can do nothing without the Father, for it is the Father that does these things. The Son is the instrument through which all is accomplished. *(John 5:19)* The Father does not reconsider what the Christ chooses to do; they are of like mind, and the Father will do all that the Christ wants done for the sake of mankind.

Just like any human, Christ gets hungry and eats. *(Mark 11:12* and *Luke 7:34)* Gods do not get hungry. More evidence that Christ was a man, and not a God is found in *John 10:29 & 30.* This passage explains how the Father and Christ are One. It is this unity that makes all the miracles possible. Christ also tells how He and the Father are separate in the handling of things.

Other passages illustrating how the Father works through the Son are found in the stories of healing in *Mark 5:8–32* and *Luke 8:43-48.* In the latter, Jesus is in a crowd, and someone touches his robe. He feels a rush of power go through him and wants to know who touched him. The disciples are not aware of what has happened, and no one has looked to Jesus for help. Then a woman comes forth and exclaims that it was she who touched His robe and was healed.

The Father had taken it upon himself to help this woman because of her great faith. This reveals the Father as the actual performer of the miracle and Christ as the vehicle through which all things are accomplished. In *John 14:10,* Christ says the Father doeth the works.

God's power flows through Jesus as evidenced in *John 5:30* "I can of mine own self do nothing: as I hear, I judge: and my judgment is just; because I seek not mine own will, but the will of the Father which hath sent me." Jesus says in *John 14:24* ". . . the word which ye hear is not mine, but the Father's which sent me."

In the story of the woman who is healed by touching the hem of the robe of Jesus (*Luke 8:43-48* and *Mark 5:25–28*), Jesus feels the power of healing being transmitted through him even before he sees the woman who needs healing. The Almighty does not need Christ's permission to do a deed for some one, but Christ must get the power from the Almighty to do a blessing. They are not one, or this would not be the case.

An incident takes place at the Temple in Jerusalem when Jesus is twelve years old. Joseph and Mary have gone to Jerusalem to celebrate Passover. Jesus, the Son, is occupied with His Father's business, absorbed in asking questions of the teachers. He is so absorbed, in fact, that he does not tell his mother when he stays behind and she does not immediately realize He is not with her. The authors of the Gospels may have dropped a hint of His humanity in this not unusual pre-adolescent behavior of His not telling His mother when he stayed behind.

Until the time of the wedding at Cana, Jesus lived an ordinary life. But then this mortal man from Nazareth was able to make wine from water. The cat was out of the bag.

The Wedding at Cana. There is a large wedding at Cana to which Jesus and his five disciples (Andrew, Simon Peter, Phillip, Nathanael, and an unnamed man), as well as Mariam, are invited. The many guests have been having a good time and have extinguished the wine supply. The mother comes to Jesus and says to Him, "They have no wine." Jesus rebels. "It is not my fault they do not have wine. It is not time for me to start my ministry." But the mother has a big footprint in this story, and He give in and does as he is told. The wedding is blessed with about 100 gallons of good wine. This was the first of the many signs through which Jesus revealed his glory.

From the negative way Christ initially responded to his mother at the wedding at Cana, do you harbor any thoughts that Jesus may have been human while here on earth?

Just How Much Wine?

How much wine did Jesus create from water? A lot! There were 6 water pots. Each pot could hold 2 to 3 firkins. A firkin is about 9 gallons. That means there were between 108 to 162 gallons of wine. Can we assume that the guests had already consumed as much as Jesus created? It must have been quite a party!

There is much in these verses that goes unsaid. We shall start at the end of the narrative and go through the verses. New wine has a bad reputation in the Bible. This wine is aged and of good quality, the wine of pleasure, appropriate for a wedding.

John 2:2–10 (King James Version)

2. Jesus was called, and his disciples, to the marriage
3. And when they had depleted the wine, the mother of Jesus saith unto Him, they have no wine.
4. Jesus saith unto her, Woman what have I to do with thee? Mine hour hast not yet come.
5. His mother saith unto the servants whatsoever He saith unto you, do it.
6. And there were set there six water pots of stone, after the manner of the purifying of the Jews, containing two or three firkins apiece.
7. Jesus saith unto them, fill the water pots with water. They filled them to the brim.
8. And he saith unto them, Draw out now, and bear unto the governor of the feast. And they bear it.
9. And when the ruler of the feast had tasted the water that was made wine, and knew not whence it was, (but the servants which drew the water knew;) the governor of the feast called the bridegroom.
10. And saith unto him, Every man at the beginning doth set forth good wine, and when the men have drunk, then that which is worse : but thou hast kept the good wine until now.

Were the servants able to sleep well that night, after seeing a couple of barrels of wine made in front of their eyes? More surprising is that after replying to his Mother in a negative manner, He went ahead and produced the wine just as she had instructed. What changed his mind? The mother of Jesus must also have been aware of her power.

From the negative way Christ initially responded to his mother at the wedding, do you harbor any thoughts that Jesus may have been human while here on earth?

What's important here is how the miracle was performed. First, Jesus had to decide to do it. If Jesus had a mind to do it, then the Almighty would supply the power to complete the request. We have no evidence that an angel spoke to either the mother or to Jesus. That implies that to Jesus his mother had great power. But it also meant that his mother knew the right time for Him to begin His ministry, this ministry from heaven that was revealed when John the Baptist leapt in his mother's womb. John, the reincarnated Abel, fully aware of the planned ministry, knew that the plan was now in progress.

By this time Jesus and his mother had moved to Capernaum and had a house there. Joseph had most likely passed away. The Jewish people in Mariam's family did not have any responsibility for her care and upkeep. This was her Son's job. Some passages reflect that His mother spent a considerable amount of time with Jesus in His mission to save the world.

The surname of more than one of the disciples, Alphaeus, is indicative of their relationship to Jesus. With this knowledge, perhaps that is why many of the family followed Christ. There were individuals from Joseph's family that followed, and some from the sister Mary's family. The report that Jesus did not sin would cast him in a very different light from ordinary people.

Did the people who were at The Last Supper recognize from the time Jesus was a young boy that he had extraordinary gifts? Even before he was performing miracles, they must have known he was different. The Baptist certainly recognized Jesus when he saw Him. But the family and the disciples did *not* apparently look upon him as God. They called him Master or Rabbi, meaning teacher. Gods do not eat bread and drink wine. Mortals do. Mortals do not have the power to kill Gods. But Christ died on the cross.

Jesus in *John 5:19* says that he can do nothing except through power from the Father. In *John 5:22*, the Father has given Jesus the unrestricted power to judge where to do the work. The Father does not question any act that Jesus wants to do.

The Biblical passages make a good argument for there being two personalities in the narrative. There is the Holy Ghost on the left hand of God and Jesus sitting on the right hand. (*Luke 22:69, Acts 2:33,* and *Colossians 3:1)* Jesus does whatever he chooses, and the Holy Ghost relates to you what the Holy Ghost hears. (*John 16:13)* Again wearing the humble title of puppet, the Holy Ghost and the Son of God do what God dictates.

Although they were cousins, John the Baptist and Jesus did not spend time together as youths. Nevertheless, the Baptist recognized Jesus when he approached him for baptism. This recognition was confirmed when the dove landed on the head of Jesus. (*John 1:31 and 32)*

When Jesus returned the next day, John the Baptist told two of his followers that Jesus was the Lamb of God. *(John 1:33-36)* After hearing Jesus speak, the followers took leave of the Baptist and followed Jesus. These two were Andrew and another follower of John the Baptist. *(John 1:40-41)*

When the Christ sees Peter the first time, He renames him Cephas, which means rock *(John 1:42)*, later referred to as "the rock on which I build my church." The next day Jesus goes up to Galilee and acquires another disciple, Phillip. *(John 1:43)* Phillip is from the same town as Andrew and Simon Peter. Phillip then recruits his friend Nathan. By the time Christ arrives for the wedding at Cana, he has five disciples.

That Jesus was human, with all the human attributes, seems to me to be irrefutable. To begin with, the narrative of Jesus, as a man, starts at the conception. As we said earlier, Mortals arrive here through the birth canal, but Gods do not. Also, mortals cannot kill Gods, and Christ died on the cross.

Continue to another passage in which John the Baptist received instructions from The Almighty. *(John 1:33)* "He that sent me to baptize with water, the same said unto me, Upon whom thou shalt see the Spirit descending, and remaining on him, the same is he which baptizeth with the Holy Ghost." John the Baptist is very clear that he, John was sent here to be the forerunner of the Messiah. In addition to the Apostle John's words, we have *Luke 3:22, Mark 1:10 & 11* and *Matthew 3:13-16.*

The veracity of this narrative is confirmed by the fact that all four Apostles recorded this scene independently. The Voice proclaims that this is indeed the Son of God.

Here are Jesus' own words establishing that He does not think that he is God. *John 1:14, John 5:30, John 14:24,* and *John 5 :23* all present Jesus as a human.

- *John 8:29* "He that sent me is with me, the Father hath not left me alone: for I do always those things that please Him." (This is the type of Father and Son relationship we honor.)
- *John 5:26 & 27:* "For as the Father hath life in Himself, so hath He given to the Son to have life in himself. And hath given Him authority to execute judgment also, because he is the son of man." (Jesus is better to judge man because he has walked in man's shoes for a better perspective of man's situation here on earth.)

- *John 5:30:* "I can of mine own self, do nothing: as I hear, I judge: and my judgment is just, because I seek not mine own will, but the will if the Father which hath sent me."
- *Luke 10:22:* "All things are delivered to me of my Father, and no man knoweth who the son is, but the Father."
- *Matthew 11:27:* "All things are delivered unto me of my Father: and no man knoweth the son, but the Father."
- *John 12:49:* "For I have not spoken of my self, but the Father which sent me, He gave me a commandment what I should say and what I should speak."
- *Luke 7:34:* "The son of man is come eating and drinking: and ye say, behold a gluttonous man, and a winebibber, a friend of publicans and sinners."
- *John 5:22:* "For the Father judgeth no man, but hath committed all judgment unto the son."
- *John 3:35:* "The Father loveth the son, and hath given all things unto his hand."
- *Luke 5:14:* "And he charged him to tell no man: but go, and show thyself to the priest."
- *Luke 9:21:* "And he straitly charged them, and commanded them to tell no man that thing."
- *John 8:56:* "And her parents were astonished: but he charged them that they should tell no man what was done."
- *Luke 4:41:* "And the devils came out of many, crying out, and saying, Thou art Christ the son of God. And he rebuking them suffered them not to speak: for they knew that he was the Christ."

Docetism

Docetism is a belief that Jesus the Christ is God. For further proof that this interpretation is in error, think about how God reacted to Lucifer's thinking that he should be the one in command. *"I the lord thy god, am a jealous god."* This comment should make it clear that the person in Power is not relinquishing the chair to anyone. Not even to His only Son.

Hebrews 2:7 & 9: Christ is described as lower than angels.

The best evidence is the words of Christ himself. *(Matthew 26: 64, Luke 16:19,* and *Mark 14:62)*

The following passages all contain the words, "Him that sent me:" *John 6:38, John 8:26 & 27, John 12: 49,* and *John 5:30*

Docetism

Docetism is broadly defined as any teaching that claims that Jesus' body was either absent or illusory.

In Christian terminology, docetism (from the Greek δοκεῖν/δόκησις dokeîn (to seem) /dókēsis (apparition, phantom), according to Norbert Brox,[1] is defined narrowly as "the doctrine according to which the phenomenon of Christ, his historical and bodily existence, and thus above all the human form of Jesus, was altogether mere semblance without any true reality." Broadly it is taken as the belief that Jesus only seemed to be human, and that his human form was an illusion. The word Δοκηταί Dokētaí (illusionists) referring to early groups who denied Jesus' humanity, first occurred in a letter by Bishop Serapion of Antioch (197–203), who discovered the doctrine in the Gospel of Peter, during a pastoral visit to a Christian community using it in Rhosus, and later condemned it as a forgery. It appears to have arisen over theological contentions concerning the meaning, figurative or literal, of a sentence from the Gospel of John: "the Word was made Flesh".

Docetism was unequivocally rejected at the First Council of Nicaea in 325 and is regarded as heretical by the Catholic Church, Orthodox Church, and Coptic Church.

Wikipedia

---

1   Norbert Brox (✶ 23 June 1935 in Paderborn ; † 30 September 2006 in Freiburg im Breisgau) was a German Catholic theologian. He was Professor of Ancient Church History and Patristic Studies and Professor of Historical Theology at the University of Regensburg .

It is clear from *Matthew 24:36* and *Mark 13:32* that the Father knows that Christ does not know the end time because the Father has not told Christ, further evidence of a separation of individuals.

Christ works under the power of The Almighty. My understanding of Christ's place is that it is similar to a puppet. The Father pulls all the strings. In my imagination, this power feels something like when you are holding the water hose, and your friend turns on the water. You can feel the water's presence and the pressure on the hose. This is the feeling of power that I imagine Christ had when he performed miracles.

In conclusion, Christ is connecting with The Father as part of the Triune Godhead, sitting on God's right hand.

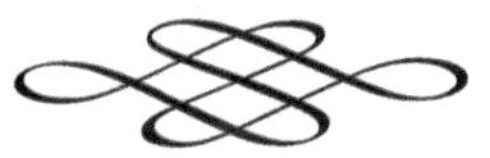

Chapter 10
Ascension Day - It Is Up To You

Christ's Last Day. Christ's last day on earth was observed by many of the disciples, about a hundred and twenty by Peter's count. *(Acts 1:10-26)* In this passage, there are two men in white standing with the throng, and they tell the group to go back to Jerusalem. The passage does not allude to these men ascending with Christ. The passage gives no hint as to who they were. Moses and Elijah were there on Transfiguration Day. The disciples saw and recognized Moses and Elijah, but did not name these two men.

Moses and Elijah (Elias) appear in three of the gospels. In *Mark 9:4* and *Matthew 17:3* Elias and Moses are talking with Jesus. Why did they come to Jesus at that time.? In *Luke 9:30* the three speak of Jesus' departure from this life. It is a prelude to what we will find in the following passages describing Jesus in the garden at Gethsemane: *Mark 14:33-42* and *Matthew 26:36-46.*

These passages will reveal to you that Christ asked His Father to take the bitter cup from Him. The earlier meeting with Moses and Elias was to inform Christ that He had to go through with God's plan, and die on the cross in Jerusalem.

There are only nine verses in Acts that say that Jesus stayed on earth for forty days after He had risen from the dead. Although it is not written, it is likely that the disciples partook of the omophagia ritual at every evening meal. This is God's promise, not that of Jesus.

It was the custom for Pilate to release a prisoner. *(John 18:39)* The Jews did not want Jesus. He had to be crucified to fulfill the scriptures. *(Matthew 27:2)* The trial of Christ ended with the Jews getting Barabbas set free in exchange for Christ.

The women came early in the morn to prepare Jesus for burial. They found the stone in the door rolled away and a young man sitting on the right side. The young man said, "He is risen." The women returned to the disciples and told them that Christ was risen. *(Mark 16:14)*

Up to that time, Pilate had found Jesus to be free from a sentence for some transgression. However, the Jewish High Priests had it in for Christ, as Jesus had thrown the peddlers and moneylenders out of the synagogue. It was a house of God, not a marketplace.

Jesus had just ridden into Jerusalem on the back of an ass. This was appropriate, for in his mother's womb, He had ridden to His birth on the back of an ass. Herod and Pilate had become friendly, as Herod had desired to visit Christ, for he had heard of many good things Christ had done. Also came a priestly Jew, Nicodemus, with a hundred pound weight of myrrh and aloes to embalm Jesus. *(John 19:39)* Nicodemus came with Joseph of Arimathaea to put His body in Joseph's new tomb. *(John 19:38)* It is not common knowledge, but criminals were hanged naked. They took His clothes and cast lots for them because His robe was of one piece. *(Luke 23:34 and Matthew 27:35)*

The Sabbath was beginning, and it was necessary to have Golgotha cleared of criminals. Christ had told the other criminal that He and this criminal who liked Jesus would be in Paradise today, as soon as the crucifixion was over. The criminal would not have to wait until Peter opened his book of life to see if the criminal's name was in the book. In *Luke 23:43* Christ tells the criminal, "Today shalt thou be in paradise." The criminal had followed the rules to gain a berth in heaven when he died. There must be some rule for the Christians to learn. Had it been revealed? Read the chapter on the requirements to get into Heaven to find out.

Christ was made to carry His personal Cross to Golgotha. He was assisted by Simon, a Cyrenian. Where were His faithful disciples? Hiding in the upper room. In the trials and tribulations of Christ at this time there were no Apostles noted as being on the job.

Who were the individuals at the cross with Jesus? Who was at The Last Supper? There are several possibilities. Important factors in determining the answer are the timing and the surnames of various people.

Acts 1:13-15 reports that about 120 people were in the room during The Last Supper. In the Acts account, the Virgin Mother was there with the disciples. What happened to her afterwards? Who took care of her? The Last Supper was held in an upper room. It's not likely they had rooms all over town to stay in.

Who was the beloved who took Jesus mother in? In *John 19:26 & 27*, John wrote, "The one Jesus loved took his mother to his home from that day on." Several people would qualify as "the one Jesus loved."

What generates considerable controversy is the giving of the Mother of Him into the care of a disciple after the hanging. The Mother of Him was about twenty at the birth of Jesus. So at the time of the crucifixion, about thirty-three years later, she would be close to fifty-three years old. The Apostle John was in close proximity during the next three years as the movement of Christianity grew. This would have allowed the Apostle John to be the beloved one to accept the mother of Him.

But I don't think it was John. Here's why. First, there are the passages that state that all of the sheep i.e. the apostles, scattered, leaving Jesus alone. *(Psalm 88:8, Zechariah 13:7, Matthew 26:56,* and *Mark 14:27)* My adamant position is that the Bible is true. There are no doubts about the intent of the passages. One can assume their interpretation is correct. Several passages with the same and or similar content appearing in both the Old Testament and the New Testament should be the guiding light for the final decision.

In *John 19:27*, the disciple takes the mother of Him into to his home. Since the Apostle John did stay in the area for the next twelve years, this invites idea that he might have had a home for the Virgin Mother. The only real Biblical evidence that makes me think that the Apostle John was not at the cross comes from Jesus saying that the apostles would all abandon Him that night and the next day. The disciples were not anywhere near the street where Jesus had to carry the cross to Golgotha. They surely must have known that He would need some assistance. Not one apostle brags that he was there for Christ at the cross. *(Luke 23:49)* They all forsook Him and fled. *(Mark 14:50)*

There is no mention in several Bible passages that the persons at the cross included any of the Apostles, although several women are mentioned. In The Book of John, there were also acquaintances mentioned.

In the story of Lazarus in the Book of John, the love of Jesus for Lazarus is noted. This extended narrative on Lazarus, the emphasis on the depth of love, and the fact that the story is in the Book of John, is considerable evidence that the Savior loved this man. Bringing Lazarus back to life made Lazarus available to take care of His mother. Note that it was the custom of the Jewish people for the children to take care of the adults. But in Christ's case, there were no other children to take on that responsibility.

It seems that John wanted everyone to know that Jesus loved him. When Mary Magdalene announced that the stone closing up the sepulcher had been rolled away, John even seemed to make a point of outrunning Peter, beating him to the sepulcher. It is probable that he outran Peter because he was younger. Now we know that old Peter was the oldest disciple. But not decrepit. *(John 13:23 -25* and *John 20:2)*

Psalm 88:8, Mark 14:22, and *Mark 14:40* indicate that the disciples were not at the cross; all eleven were gone.

Christ had to save Lazarus to take care of his mother. How can you think that Christ loved a boy more than He did a man he *raised from the dead?* You do not know. However, I will allow you to *believe* that Christ loved the boy more that he did the man. Well, I'm proselytizing here, which is not acceptable in my own philosophy.

To continue our search for who was at the cross, *Mark 15:40* lists Mary Magdalene, Mary the mother of the younger James, and Salome. In *Matthew 27:56-61,* we have again Mary Magdalene and the other Mary, the mother of James and Joseph. This "other Mary" is the long-time follower from Galilee.

John 19:25 lists these persons at the cross: His mother, the Virgin Mother's sister, Mary the wife of Cleophas, and Mary Magdalene. The next individual the apostle mentions is the favorite follower of the Christ. Remember that it is stated in several passages, that none, *none,* of the apostles were at the cross. That leaves Lazarus as the beloved friend at the cross who accepted responsibility for Jesus' virgin mother.

The Story of Lazarus

John 11:1-45 (King James Version)

1. Now a certain man was sick, named Lazarus, of Bethany, the town of Mary and her sister Martha.
2. (It was that Mary which anointed the Lord with ointment, and wiped his feet with her hair, whose brother Lazarus was sick.)
3. Therefore his sisters sent unto him, saying, Lord, behold, he whom thou lovest is sick.
4. When Jesus heard that, he said, This sickness is not unto death, but for the glory of God, that the Son of God might be glorified thereby.
5. Now Jesus loved Martha, and her sister, and Lazarus.
6. When he had heard therefore that he was sick, he abode two days still in the same place where he was.
7. Then after that saith he to his disciples, Let us go into Judaea again.
8. His disciples say unto him, Master, the Jews of late sought to stone thee; and goest thou thither again?
9. Jesus answered, Are there not twelve hours in the day? If any man walk in the day, he stumbleth not, because he seeth the light of this world.
10. But if a man walk in the night, he stumbleth, because there is no light in him.
11. These things said he: and after that he saith unto them, Our friend Lazarus sleepeth; but I go, that I may awake him out of sleep.
12. Then said his disciples, Lord, if he sleep, he shall do well.
13. Howbeit Jesus spake of his death: but they thought that he had spoken of taking of rest in sleep.
14. Then said Jesus unto them plainly, Lazarus is dead.
15. And I am glad for your sakes that I was not there, to the intent ye may believe; nevertheless let us go unto him.
16. Then said Thomas, which is called Didymus, unto his fellow disciples, Let us also go, that we may die with him.
17. Then when Jesus came, he found that he had lain in the grave four days already.
18. Now Bethany was nigh unto Jerusalem, about fifteen furlongs off:
19. And many of the Jews came to Martha and Mary, to comfort them concerning their brother.
20. Then Martha, as soon as she heard that Jesus was coming, went and met him: but Mary sat still in the house.
21. Then said Martha unto Jesus, Lord, if thou hadst been here, my brother had not died.
22. But I know, that even now, whatsoever thou wilt ask of God, God will give it thee.
23. Jesus saith unto her, Thy brother shall rise again.

24. Martha saith unto him, I know that he shall rise again in the resurrection at the last day.

25. Jesus said unto her, I am the resurrection, and the life: he that believeth in me, though he were dead, yet shall he live:

26. And whosoever liveth and believeth in me shall never die. Believest thou this?

27. She saith unto him, Yea, Lord: I believe that thou art the Christ, the Son of God, which should come into the world.

28. And when she had so said, she went her way, and called Mary her sister secretly, saying, The Master is come, and calleth for thee.

29. As soon as she heard that, she arose quickly, and came unto him.

30. Now Jesus was not yet come into the town, but was in that place where Martha met him.

31. The Jews then which were with her in the house, and comforted her, when they saw Mary, that she rose up hastily and went out, followed her, saying, She goeth unto the grave to weep there.

32. Then when Mary was come where Jesus was, and saw him, she fell down at his feet, saying unto him, Lord, if thou hadst been here, my brother had not died.

33. When Jesus therefore saw her weeping, and the Jews also weeping which came with her, he groaned in the spirit, and was troubled.

34. And said, Where have ye laid him? They said unto him, Lord, come and see.

35. Jesus wept.

36. Then said the Jews, Behold how he loved him!

37. And some of them said, Could not this man, which opened the eyes of the blind, have caused that even this man should not have died?

38. Jesus therefore again groaning in himself cometh to the grave. It was a cave, and a stone lay upon it.

39. Jesus said, Take ye away the stone. Martha, the sister of him that was dead, saith unto him, Lord, by this time he stinketh: for he hath been dead four days.

40. Jesus saith unto her, Said I not unto thee, that, if thou wouldest believe, thou shouldest see the glory of God?

41. Then they took away the stone from the place where the dead was laid. And Jesus lifted up his eyes, and said, Father, I thank thee that thou hast heard me.

42. And I knew that thou hearest me always: but because of the people which stand by I said it, that they may believe that thou hast sent me.

43. And when he thus had spoken, he cried with a loud voice, Lazarus, come forth.

44. And he that was dead came forth, bound hand and foot with grave clothes: and his face was bound about with a napkin. Jesus saith unto them, Loose him, and let him go.

45. Then many of the Jews which came to Mary, and had seen the things which Jesus did, believed on him.

The story of the early gathering of disciples has two versions. Matthew and Mark mostly agree, but Luke and John have a different version. That is not what we are about to discuss. Our focus is the study of John, beloved of Christ.

In *Luke 3:23*, the Christ is about thirty years old. The apostle John is about ten years his junior. John the beloved deeply admires Jesus for his a life of celibacy. The other members of Christ's church have wives, family, and children. This is fine, but at that young age it would not be likely that John had a house or a home.

Reading the scripture carefully, we note that the Apostle John was held close to the bosom of Jesus at the Last Supper. The crowd at the raising of Lazarus observed how much Jesus loved Lazarus. So which is it to be?

It is important for the follower to ferret out exactly which follower was at the cross to accept responsibility for caring for the mother of Him. Your faith now faces the question. Do you believe the Bible, or do you follow your own interpretation?

Relating to the Old Testament writing New Testament: *Psalm 88:8, Mark 14:27,* and *Zechariah 13:5–7* all refer to the scattering of the sheep, to the abandonment of Jesus by His friends.

There are no passages that will turn this around. That relegates the job of taking care of His mother to Lazarus. We will add to that the observation that the Apostle John was very young by his own account in *John 20:2.* John brags about his being the one beloved by Jesus and then brags some more about his ability to outrun ol' Peter to the sepulcher. That denotes his youth. Besides, having followed Jesus for the past three years, how would he have had the wherewithal to lay up money for housing and sustenance for some old lady of 53?

The Last Supper, a Mystery. Mariam is in the Upper Room to attend the Last Supper. There Jesus washes the feet of the apostles. Bishop Fulton Sheen noted that Jesus even washed the feet of Judas. All 12 disciples had their feet washed that night, possibly all 120 believers who had gathered. But it seems Jesus didn't wash His mother's feet. Surely His Father would have Him wash His mother's feet. This remains an unsolved mystery in my mind.

The Resurrection. In the description of the Resurrection in *Luke 24:39–42*, the Christ has entered again into His earthly body and can eat and drink, like a human and not a spirit. In *Luke 24:13–53* two followers meet Jesus in the village of Emmaus, but they do not recognize him. (After all, they think he is dead.) It is late, and thinking Jesus is a stranger, they invite him to stay with them. When he blesses their meal, their eyes are opened. They see who he is and are filled with joy.

In *John 20:19* Jesus, supposedly dead, makes another surprise appearance:

"Then the same day at evening, being the first day of the week, when the doors were shut where the disciples were assembled for fear of the Jews, came Jesus and stood in the midst, and saith unto them, Peace be unto you."

In the end, it is up to *you*. Luke 12:39–47: *"Be prepared for you know not when Christ is coming."*

Chapter 11
Requirements for Entry into Heaven

The requirements for entry into Heaven do not vary. To believe, to be born again and to partake of communion are all that are required to gain entrance to heaven. (As I sit here and cogitate on these matters, the energy that it takes to get back to heaven seems nearly ridiculous.)

"With all thy getting, get thee wisdom and understanding," is fairly straightforward advice. *(Proverbs 4:7)* The Bible repeatedly exhorts you to be a follower of God in thought, word and deeds. The problem is that the deeds portion can be very challenging. *Psalm 42:8* is a confirmation of the beauty of the relationship with the Lord. "Yet the Lord will command his loving-kindness in the day time, and in the night his song shall be with me, and my prayer unto the God of my life."

Jesus is the Redeemer, and the ones He is searching for are the lost host from heaven. In *Luke 14* Jesus talks about forsaking social and familial relationships to follow Him. This is one of the most difficult passages in the New Testament, and it must be read in context of the whole chapter to begin to understand the meaning. There are many excellent analyses of this chapter, which fundamentally is about what you must do to regain your heavenly soul.

Celibacy as a Tool. Celibacy, learning to listen to the voice within, and being able to say from your very core, "I BELIEVE," are tools that will enable you to be born again and achieve true communion. Your intent must have considerable force, weight, and just plain belief that can be judged as true intent. This cannot be seen by the outsider, but to God and the believer, it is an action.

Luke, Chapter 14 (King James Version)

1. And it came to pass, as he went into the house of one of the chief Pharisees to eat bread on the sabbath day, that they watched him.

2. And, behold, there was a certain man before him which had the dropsy.

3. And Jesus answering spake unto the lawyers and Pharisees, saying, Is it lawful to heal on the sabbath day?

4. And they held their peace. And he took him, and healed him, and let him go;

5. And answered them, saying, Which of you shall have an ass or an ox fallen into a pit, and will not straightway pull him out on the sabbath day?

6. And they could not answer him again to these things.

7. And he put forth a parable to those which were bidden, when he marked how they chose out the chief rooms; saying unto them.

8. When thou art bidden of any man to a wedding, sit not down in the highest room; lest a more honourable man than thou be bidden of him;

9. And he that bade thee and him come and say to thee, Give this man place; and thou begin with shame to take the lowest room.

10. But when thou art bidden, go and sit down in the lowest room; that when he that bade thee cometh, he may say unto thee, Friend, go up higher: then shalt thou have worship in the presence of them that sit at meat with thee.

11. For whosoever exalteth himself shall be abased; and he that humbleth himself shall be exalted.

12. Then said he also to him that bade him, When thou makest a dinner or a supper, call not thy friends, nor thy brethren, neither thy kinsmen, nor thy rich neighbours; lest they also bid thee again, and a recompence be made thee.

13. But when thou makest a feast, call the poor, the maimed, the lame, the blind:

14. And thou shalt be blessed; for they cannot recompense thee: for thou shalt be recompensed at the resurrection of the just.

15. And when one of them that sat at meat with him heard these things, he said unto him, Blessed is he that shall eat bread in the kingdom of God.

16. Then said he unto him, A certain man made a great supper, and bade many:

17. And sent his servant at supper time to say to them that were bidden, Come; for all things are now ready.

18. And they all with one consent began to make excuse. The first said unto him, I have bought a piece of ground, and I must needs go and see it: I pray thee have me excused.

19. And another said, I have bought five yoke of oxen, and I go to prove them: I pray thee have me excused.

20. And another said, I have married a wife, and therefore I cannot come.

21. So that servant came, and shewed his lord these things. Then the master of the house being angry said to his servant, Go out quickly into the streets and lanes of the city, and bring in hither the poor, and the maimed, and the halt, and the blind.

22. And the servant said, Lord, it is done as thou hast commanded, and yet there is room.

23. And the lord said unto the servant, Go out into the highways and hedges, and compel them to come in, that my house may be filled.

24. For I say unto you, That none of those men which were bidden shall taste of my supper.

25. And there went great multitudes with him: and he turned, and said unto them,

26. If any man come to me, and hate not his father, and mother, and wife, and children, and brethren, and sisters, yea, and his own life also, he cannot be my disciple.

27. And whosoever doth not bear his cross, and come after me, cannot be my disciple.

28. For which of you, intending to build a tower, sitteth not down first, and counteth the cost, whether he have sufficient to finish it?

29. Lest haply, after he hath laid the foundation, and is not able to finish it, all that behold it begin to mock him,

30. Saying, This man began to build, and was not able to finish.

31. Or what king, going to make war against another king, sitteth not down first, and consulteth whether he be able with ten thousand to meet him that cometh against him with twenty thousand?

32. Or else, while the other is yet a great way off, he sendeth an ambassage, and desireth conditions of peace.

33. So likewise, whosoever he be of you that forsaketh not all that he hath, he cannot be my disciple.

34. Salt is good: but if the salt have lost his savour, wherewith shall it be seasoned?

35. It is neither fit for the land, nor yet for the dunghill; but men cast it out. He that hath ears to hear, let him hear.

Of course with your earthly soul, you are actually *re-entering* Heaven. Concerning the requirement of being born again, Nicodemus exclaimed, "How do I go back to my mother's womb?" This is accomplished by reversing God's command be fruitful and multiply by becoming a eunuch if you are a man or a virgin if you are a woman.

Christ in *Matthew 19:12* mentions the eunuch five times. In *Acts 8:27, 34, 36, 38 & 39,* the eunuch is again mentioned five times. (In both cases, the number is five: numerology again.) *Strong's Concordance to the Bible,* in defining eunuch, does not make any reference to abstaining from sex or celibacy; the definition is CLEAN. *"Create in me a clean heart, oh God, and renew the right spirit within me."*

This necessary ingredient for claiming a spot in heaven is very simple. For the man, it is the regeneration of the pineal gland. This stringent requirement is written about in many books and in many languages. All it takes to be born again and get to heaven is for the man to work on hardening of the pineal gland, and for the women to have their hymen replaced.

The Pineal Gland and the Third Eye. The purpose of the development of the pineal gland is to reach the goal of the philosopher's stone. It takes thirteen moons. To further clarify the essence of the stone, the pineal gland is the Rock on which God will build His church. Jesus says to Peter, "On this rock I will build my church. *(Matthew 16:18)* In Theosophy and some other philosophies, the rock is equated to the enhanced pineal gland, a third eye.

This would also be the mode, the time capsule, for the woman to fulfill the time required to re-enter heaven at the end of life here on earth. Of those that are given much, much shall be required. *(Luke 12:48)*

It is told that the eunuchs of old increased in wisdom and knowledge and gained positions of honor in harems and government. The secret is the retention of the seminal fluid, which has the propensity to charge the pineal gland. This charges the third eye, which is able to see everything.

The Third Eye

The third eye (also known as the inner eye) is a mystical and esoteric concept referring to a speculative invisible eye which provides perception beyond ordinary sight. In Theosophy it is related to the pineal gland. The third eye refers to the gate that leads to inner realms and spaces of higher consciousness. The third eye is often associated with religious visions, clairvoyance, the ability to observe chakras and auras, precognition, and out-of-body experiences.

Wikipedia

A Cambodian Shiva head showing a third eye.

89

The Eye of Horus

The Eye of Horus is an ancient Egyptian symbol of protection, royal power and good health. The eye is personified in the goddess Wadjet (also written as Wedjat, or Udjat, Uadjet, Wedjoyet, Edjo or Uto). It is also known as "The Eye of Ra".

The name Wadjet is derived from "wadj" meaning "green", hence "the green one", and was known to the Greeks and Romans as "uraeus" from the Egyptian "iaret" meaning "risen one" from the image of a cobra rising up in protection.

Funerary amulets were often made in the shape of the Eye of Horus. The Wadjet or Eye of Horus is "the central element" of seven "gold, faience, carnelian and lapis lazuli" bracelets found on the mummy of Shoshenq II. The Wedjat "was intended to protect the pharaoh in the afterlife" and to ward off evil. Ancient Egyptian and Near Eastern sailors would frequently paint the symbol on the bow of their vessel to ensure safe sea travel.

The Eye of Horus is sometimes called the Eye of Providence and is found on the reverse side of every dollar bill. Wikipedia

The ancient Egyptian concept of the Eye of Horus is helpful. The list of sources of information about it is long, but perusal of the material will bring you considerable mirth and joy after you have received the Celestial Spark.

In Egyptian mythology, the argument of who would be king, Set or Horus, was settled by semen. The semen of Set came out of the top of his head as a golden disk. In *Acts 2:2-4*, the Holy Ghost appeared to the disciples as a flame of fire sitting upon them, presumably on the top of their heads. This is the location of the pineal and pituitary glands.

The coals of fire on the disciple's head are emanating from the pineal gland that is alive from retaining the seminal fluid. For the women it is the pituitary gland, enlivened by the replacement of the hymen.

Celibacy is the desired avenue for the pilgrim to follow. This is to imply that the sex act is out of character for one to be righteous in the eyes of the Almighty.

We will start with King David, and how he handled this matter. David had six wives. He acquired two of the wives by having the husband killed. In addition to the six wives, David had ten concubines to work in the temple. In the end, when David was getting on in years, the sons threw the prettiest girl in all of Israel into the King's bed. The King did not respond in the usual manner, and the sons thought of him as dead. *(1 Kings 1:1–4)*

In the stories, the Almighty held King David in high esteem, with his six wives and ten concubines. King David's refusal of the maiden indicates that celibacy is the path for the disciple to follow.

Absalom may have been correct, that he should have been the successor to the throne. His father and mother had followed the rules of God and were man and wife, pursuing the "be fruitful and multiply" directive. Instead David has an adulterous affair with Bathsheba, who conceives out of wedlock. David has Bathsheba's husband Uriah killed by having his soldiers retreat from him during a battle.

Absalom tries to usurp the throne. King David is hiding from his son, Absalom, and plans to use false information to lure Absalom into complacency while David builds up his own forces, intending to defeat his son in battle. He pleads with his generals not to kill his son. In a stroke of irony Absalom's glorious mane of hair is caught in a tree. One of King David's generals, out for revenge, find's Absalom trapped and helpless and kills him.

David and Bathsheba's second son, Solomon, heir to the throne, builds the mighty temple in Jerusalem. He is a very wise king. But in the end, this great leader does not get the Spark and goes off and lives with his harem.

There is some force, that leads us around.

In *Genesis 38:13* we have the tale of Tamar and her father-in-law, whom she induced to seduce her by disguising herself. I find it striking that she was able to do this, but she had the assistance of estrus. Jacob had left his tools with Tamar for security on his paying for the favors. When this came to his knowledge, he acknowledged her efforts with two sons to replace the ones Jacob had lost.

Genesis 19:30–38 tells another story of seduction. Lot's two daughters seduced their father in order to keep his line going. And again estrus seems to be in play. The sex act itself is not sin. But celibacy remains the way to Heaven.

Then there is the celibacy of Christ. There are some followers who think that the wedding at Cana was that of Christ. My own view of Christ's attitude does not allow for Christ to have sex. Christ must stay on the side of His Father, as in the Garden before eating of the Tree of Truth and Knowledge. Adam and Eve went over to Satan's side of the fence.

In any reincarnation of Adam, in order to be free from all sin, the sex act could not have a part in the story. Note that there was never any effort for Jesus to leave offspring. In fact, in *Genesis 6:2* the sons of God consorting with the daughters of men was displeasing in the eyes of God. The great flood was designed to eliminate those beings from the face of the earth.

The story of Joseph and Mary (Mariam) is relevant. Joseph did not know his wife before they arrived in Bethlehem. *(Matthew 1:25)* That means that the two had not consummated the marriage. The storyteller relates that Joseph was an older man, a widower, who had children.

James the Lesser, later St. James the Lesser of the Catholic church, wrote a book that did not make it into the Holy Bible. It still exists and should be read by followers today. James records the story of the midwife Salome who determined that Mariam was a virgin. That Salome's withered hand was made whole again as she bathed the newborn babe would certainly convince Joseph that this birth was an important event indeed.

After the visit of the wise men it was again time for Joseph and Mariam to travel with the Son of God to Egypt. It would not seem likely that Joseph made this trip with an ass, Mariam, and the two year old child without some accompaniment. Perhaps his son James the Lesser accompanied them. The gifts from the Wise Men would have helped with the trip to Egypt. However, if they were to stay for any length of time, Joseph would have needed to earn some living money.

After visiting the new King, the wise men would tell Herod the location of the Child. The Wise Men did not return to Herod, and the family of Joseph moved to Egypt.

In all of this, there is no doubt in my mind that Joseph would never venture to share God's concubine. My understanding is that the shadow of the Almighty crossed over the threshold of the young lady's abode. *(Luke 1:25 and Matthew 1:18)* I do not know how you make a shadow, but for me, my body must get between me and the sun. So God's shadow in this passage is changing the girl from Satan's concubine in the garden to His own concubine for eternity. In *Genesis 3:16* God says to Eve, "in thy conception," not in the future, but right now; she is already pregnant. Adam is the first to be cuckolded.

The rules are that a mortal cannot kill a God, nor can a mortal tell a God what to do. A likely addition to the list of rules is that mortals cannot castigate a God. However, maybe I will be allowed to chide The Almighty. Keeping my place, you know. My bone to pick is this. The Almighty instructs all on the earth to be fruitful and multiply. How long one is supposed to follow this instruction is not explained or revealed. The temple of God here on earth is in the bodies of the humans, not on the corners of the streets.

Biblical References to Celibacy

- *Isaiah 56:3-5*
  "Neither let the son of the stranger, that hath joined himself to the Lord, speak,
      saying, The Lord hath utterly separated me from his people: neither let the
      eunuch say, Behold, I am a dry tree.
  For thus saith the Lord unto the eunuchs that keep my sabbaths, and choose
      the things that please me, and take hold of my covenant;
  Even unto them will I give in mine house and within my walls a place and a
      name better than of sons and of daughters: I will give them an everlasting
      name, that shall not be cut off."

- In *Jeremiah 52:25* the eunuch is a very important man. "He took also out of the
  city an eunuch, which had the charge of the men of war."

- *Matthew 19:12* "For there are some eunuchs, which were so born from their
  mother's womb: and there are some eunuchs, which were made eunuchs of
  men: and there be eunuchs, which have made themselves eunuchs for the
  kingdom of heaven's sake. He that is able to receive it, let him receive it."

- *Acts 8:27-39* tells the moving story of Philip baptizing the newly-converted
  Ethiopian eunuch.

With this revelation of the Eye of Horus, the feeding and regeneration of the pineal gland, and the concept of being born again concluded, I will now go on to discuss the woman's role.

Requirements for a Woman to Enter Heaven. In the hierarchy of souls and living persons, it is God, Man, Woman, and lastly Satan. This statement alone will cause considerable furor among many. Who committed the sin in the Garden? It was Eve led by her friend Satan. Can she, as the one who is to produce the fruit and to multiply, be saved? The answer is yes. The parable of the ten virgins in *Matthew 25* reveals how this is accomplished.

The ten virgins went to the wedding, and the groom was very late. Five of the virgins had extra oil, but the other five did not carry any reserve. When they returned with more oil, they were shut out of the wedding. (The wedding is a metaphor for heaven.) Did that mean that they were shut out heaven forever? NO. God has an open door to heaven for all who are willing to comply with the rules. Supposedly none of the ten girls had spent any time with a man, and so were considered to be virgins. The analogy of virgins with no extra oil is that they did not reveal that they had lost the hymen. The parable of not having the extra oil as the others had, is the Bible 's metaphor for the reason for the refusal of the virgins with no extra oil to enter heaven.

What needs to take place for the woman to enter into the kingdom of heaven? It is similar to the requirement for men. Both are a secret between you and God. It does not show outwardly. This secret has more meaning. It may not be God's desire for you to wear many signs and symbols bragging that you are a Christian. The real truth may be that it is only between you and Him, that you are a believer. The female can be in a position to be examined and show that she is abiding with God's plan, but the man is not able to have an examination to reveal that he is complying.

The Power of "I Believe:" The Criminal on the Cross with Jesus

Hanging on the cross, Christ is talking with the other two criminals. (They only hanged criminals in those days.) The wonderful aspect of this is that two of the criminals will be in heaven when they have passed on. One criminal had been defending Christ. The other criminal kept chiding the Christ: if He were the Son of God, why does God not save Him?

It's interesting that the proven criminal has satisfied Jesus, to the extent of passing the requirements for entrance into the kingdom heaven. *Romans 7* declares that this earthly container is a sinful body, and there is no changing or improving this it. To be born again is the requirement; no other change is necessary. You are allowed to talk dirty, have a beer and a cigar, but not to take the Lord's name in vain. Otherwise, it is wide open for you to have a good time here in Satanville.

This is almost incomprehensible, or maybe not the real story, but it comes out that way when reading and studying. Christ says He is a winebibber and a glutton. John the Baptist is murdered for being the good guy. There may be good reason for the churches not to teach this in Sunday School, as it may well be construed as Satanic.

Christ, hanging on the cross as a criminal, has examined his two companions knowingly, because He can read other minds. One of the other criminals has been born again. Christ tells him that he and Christ will be in paradise today. It is important that you be born again; when you die, you will go to heaven immediately. The big judgment so emphasized in church, is for the ones who have not been

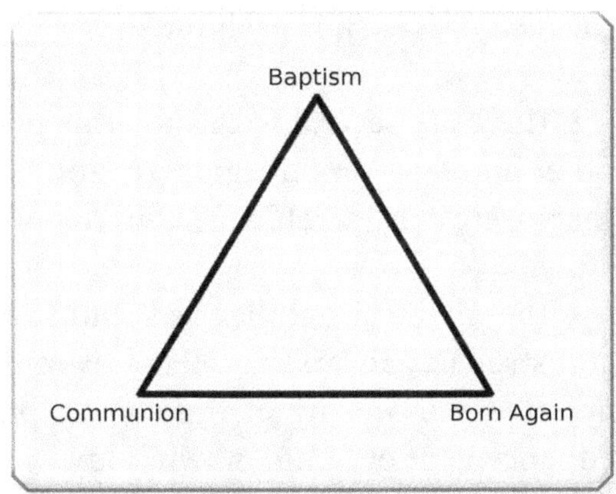

born again, but who will have an opportunity to be judged in the last days. Therefore there are two ways to get to Heaven, one is to be born again, and the other is to wait for Judgement Day.

Note that Jesus at the cross took the criminal to heaven right then. The criminal did not have to pass through the good book. This earthly sojourn is dedicated to finding the ways to heaven's entry. One way is the belief in the Christ, and the other is to be born again.

It is obvious that the criminal had passed the born again requirement, and the partaking of the sacrament of communion was not required, as it was not available. A man cannot be judged on matters necessary for admittance, when they are not available. If you are a true born again Christian and have the belief in Christ, you will be taken into heaven on your last day. You must be as a little child in your innocence and receptivity. Christ said, "Suffer the little children to come unto Me, forbid them not, for of such is the kingdom of heaven.

The Bible is full of information, but it is not presented in a regular system. You must take time and effort to study the puzzle if you are to be enlightened.

The Bible passages can have two meanings for the same words, and it is necessary for the neophyte to ferret out these nuances for better understanding of Biblical instructions. Take a walk again from the cross; Christ tells the criminal, today, not later, but right now, today. In *John 6:39, 40, 44 & 54*, you will find that if you believe in Christ, you will go to heaven today, exactly as the criminal did.

The Holy Communion. There are some serious parts of the Biblical teachings. Take the considerations on the consuming of flesh, for example. In *Strong's Concordance* there are 423 entries for the word flesh. As one goes from one passage to another, there are contradictions. In one passage consuming flesh is allowed, and in the next passage it is prohibited.

There are several words for this practice of eating flesh, specifically the flesh of other humans: omophagia, exocannibalism, endocannibilism - the list goes on as if there were considerable merit in the program.

The mythical Achilles was said to have consumed some of the flesh of his best and strongest adversaries. He was of the opinion that the great warrior he had just defeated was worthy of the consumption of some of his blood and flesh, for the enhancement of Achilles own body.

The Oregon Fish and Game Department has had a program of chumming fresh water fish with carcasses. Although there is a great effort not to violate the quality of the stream's water, the practice goes on, though for the private individual it is now illegal. The thinking in the Department is that the feeding of the fish is an enhancement to the young fish. The salmon have returned to their home breeding grounds for 10,000 years, and there was no problem with the water in those times. The salmon died after breeding, and the young fish fed on the carcasses.

The merits of eating someone's body for enhancement must have some trace of benefit, or Christ would not have included it in the sacrament at the Last Supper. Christ instructed the disciples to drink the wine and eat the bread, as it is His body and His blood. You must believe this, emphatically, to receive the desired enhancement.

The following passages are a must-read for a deeper understanding:

Matthew 26:26 & 27	*John 6:50-58*
Mark 14: 22–24	*1 Corinthians 11: 23-29*
Luke 22:19–20	

The Last Supper is very important. The ritual of communion is introduced to the congregation. It is proof that the consuming of human body and flesh will enhance the one who devours it. In the past it had been strongly against God's wishes and rules. Christ tells the disciples, "As ye eat of my body and drink my blood, do it in remembrance of me." *(Matthew 26:26)* This is one of the three rules of admission to heaven when you die.

As Ajax in Greek mythology reacted to the passing of the tools of his friend the warrior, so you must believe that these are the tools of the Messiah for your enhancement and gift. This is one of the requirements for reentry to heaven, from the bonds of Satan and earthly flesh.

Upon becoming a believer, you will not know that your belief is of any value. There is no outward confirmation or feeling to let you know you are doing the right thing. In taking communion, you *believe* that the bread and wine are truly His body and blood, and not just soup and crackers. In practicing celibacy, you *believe* that you are feeding your third eye, that you are nourishing your soul.

The holy communion is central to the idea of transformation and unity. The eating of the flesh of humans is a most interesting subject of inquiry. A query on Google turns up millions of remarks, though many of these are about the consumption of animals as food. The Old Testament if full of dietary rules, including the drinking of blood.

In *John 6:56*, Christ says, "As the living Father hath sent me, and I live by the Father: so he that eateth me, even he shall live by me." The Communion Sacrament must be of great power. It is opposite the teachings of many of the earlier passages. For the blessing of the sacrament to be effective, the partaker must wholeheartedly believe in what he is doing.

God tells you to be fruitful and multiply, but later he requires you to give up all of these earthly things to take on the mantle of Christ. Taking up the mantle of Christ means more than just saying, "I believe in Christ." Those are only words, but there is a requirement of actions on your part. If you have not been able to get the Celestial Spark, you will have your name in the book to be judged on the last day. If you are able attain the Spark, you will be as the criminal on the cross with Christ; today you will be in paradise with Him. *(John 23:43)*

Christ promises His followers that He will provide a comforter for them. This comforter is new to the followers, and will be called the Holy Ghost. The Holy Ghost is John the Baptist. *(Luke 1:41)* Abel, in the Old Testament, became John the Baptist in the New Testament. John's mother, Elisabeth, was impregnated by the Holy Ghost, which at the time was God. In the end her son, John the Baptist himself becomes the Holy Ghost, the comforter, and the voice within. *(John 7:39)*

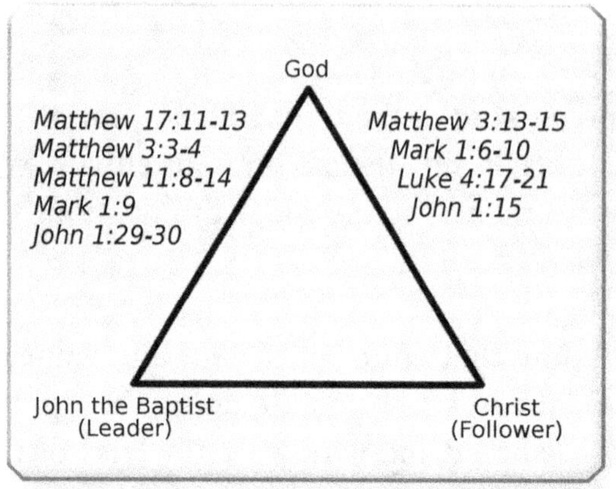

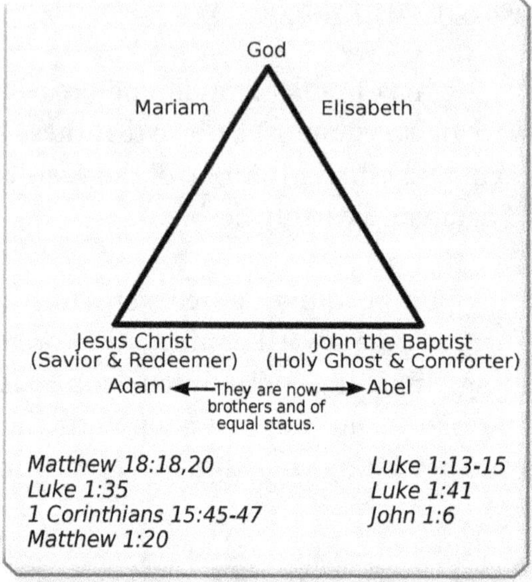

The Apostle Paul did a lot of explaining to the gentiles of the requirements for becoming a Christian. It was necessary. You will be revealed as being a Christian when you go to take the sacrament of His body and His blood.

This concludes our evidence on how to get to heaven. Remember, if you comply, you will be in heaven on your last day.

Chapter 12
On Souls, Stagnation, & The Celestial Spark

Souls. The souls from heaven are sent to earth to live in the earthly temple of your body and make an effort to get your earthling soul to listen to the voice within. The voice within is tutored by the Holy Ghost, and the message is then passed on to the body and mind of the earthling. The difficulty is that the earthling traveling down the road will arrive at a decision point. He will have to decide whether or not to continue on the paved highway to his destination. There is a problem with continuing on this paved path, and a right turn comes up on the right side. The voice within tells you to take this side road. When you hear this from the voice within, there is only just enough time to make the decision: take the turn, or stay on the paved road. The voice within is absolutely correct. It is never, ever wrong.

The heavenly soul and the earthly soul both live in the same body, also known as the earthly temple for the heavenly soul. The relationship is very strange, and it requires considerable effort by the earthling to learn to listen to the voice within.

Stagnation. Stagnation is the state of being still and not moving. It cannot be allowed in the universe. Movement is required. We may not always like it, but it is necessary. This war or strife or progress is what keeps things going and going.

A stagnant puddle gives birth to mosquitoes. Need I say more? The powers of good and evil are at odds, and knowing how the system works and why will give you considerable comfort. A good example today is technology. In the beginning it was wonderful to have all this knowledge at your fingertips. Just go on the Internet.

Before too long, the denizens of the Internet jungle started to get into your bank account without your permission. Good was very far ahead of evil in the beginning, but soon all that money changing hands made them about level again.

Another good analogy of stagnation is a house not lived in. It will deteriorate at a faster rate than if it is occupied. That may sound strange, but it is true.

Wealthy individuals contribute to the anti-stagnation, full bore. They hate taxes and welfare. They do not want the government taking money from them and handing it out to the poor, who they think do not desire to work. Just look about, and you will see a considerable effort to keep things going, for no stagnation to take place. Starvation in various places seems a little much for the anti-stagnation efforts to pursue.

Going beyond our materialistic society will take some effort. The time will come for the neophyte to recognize that his or her studies are leading the student to consider getting off this planet earth. The chaos and turmoil of existence as an earthling is more stressful than it needs to be. It is better to be a voice within and have the fun of telling the earthling to do something that may, or may not, be heeded by the listener. This most likely will be when the attraction of material things loses its power. The better things in life are free.

Getting the Spark. The neophyte wishing to gain admission to heaven must first be a believer. I BELIEVE is the first step. The next step is to be born again, and the third step is to take communion. There will be no inward feeling of certainty that confirms the feeling that you are following the rules. Your transformation is honorary and being done with your free will.

The highest hurdle of all is to believe. It is difficult. Your friends will tell you that you are nuts to believe such hogwash. There are two verses that will help: *1 Corinthians 1:21* and *1 Corinthians 4:9-10.* Review the things of God that are required to be accepted into heaven: numerology, belief in anthropophagy (as in the Holy Communion) with all its symbolism, and the retention of seminal fluid. With absolutely no proof here on earth today, it is easy for your friends to think you have lost it all. It is okay for this to be a secret and a holy mystery. Only you and your Maker need to keep track of your wisdom.

The study of metaphysics is only a hair short of staggering; it just knocks you down. It is a challenge to grasp the enormous scale of the universe in your thinking. You must ask yourself just what is there that you cannot handle, only because you do not know the answer. Some examples: subduction here on earth correlates with the black holes in the universe. The idea that the retention of the seminal fluid nourishes the pineal gland and its connection with the Eye of Horus is not easy to grasp, nor is the subtle connection of this idea to the Biblical stories of the eunuch. Science has a heavy burden, ferreting out what's behind all the wee bits of information that they are able to garner from nature.

There are a myriad of authors and stringers shouting as the muezzin from the tower cries, come with ol' Khayyam, and leave the wise to be. A good example is the Biblical tale of Saul of Tarsus who, seeing the light, became the Apostle Paul. Name change. New job. Quite a transformation. Such transformations are happening all the time, as you should be aware from this book. A strange way to reveal something is to take an unbeliever and reveal to him a story that many would not believe. It is all in the eye of the beholder. That is how those in charge do these metaphysical transformations.

A fun story from the past: Adlai Stephenson was making a speech when a supporter in the crowd rose up and proclaimed, "Governor Stevenson, every thinking person in America will vote for you!" Stevenson replied, "That's not enough. I need a majority." My advice to you? Become a thinking person. It will bring you satisfaction. Guaranteed.

By now, the naysayer will be flying out of the woodwork at these instructive words. You may tell your drinking buddies about this, but they will just laugh and laugh. So it's better that you keep it to just between you and God.

Chapter 13
Conclusion

In this closing chapter I'm a tattletale on humans. We are a sorry lot in our conduct. Greed, envy, anger, gluttony, pride, and an uncontrolled appetite for money, celebrity, and power have risen to new heights. I hope that in this book I've given you some ideas for concocting an antidote, for being born again.

I am grievously disturbed by what I see in the our society today. A democracy, by definition, is ruled by the people. We have elections, but that is about as far as we have been able to follow that ideal. The wealthy have ruled here since the inception of the nation. Debtors' prisons, in colonial times, were deplorable. Debtors were not fed nor clothed. In Connecticut, all sorts of criminals, including debtors, were held in an old mine.

Today one can declare bankruptcy and survive. The capitalistic system has been good for the USA in many ways. We have been a prosperous country. The problem is that far too many are not able or willing to share their wealth in a responsible manner. That's greed. Although some people, like Chester Carlson, the inventor of the Xerox machine, have given away virtually their entire fortunes to good works, others worth untold millions use their money to live luxuriously, to buy political influence, and to promote themselves in the media. A great deal of this effort is aimed at manipulating the crowd to vote in favor of whatever business they are involved with.

Sadly, many very large businesses here in America and around the world do not take into consideration the health of the environment. There is at this time an effort to bring an oil pipeline through the United States, and this concerns me. There is anxiety among many people about allowing this to happen in critical environmental areas when there is a potential for oil spills. The corporate entities are not listening to people's worries about running a pipeline through environmentally sensitive areas like the Sand Hills of Nebraska..

An example of something that brings me great joy are the tigers and lions and cheetahs of southeast Asia and the great plains of Africa. Those animals have not mixed up the blood; they are as pure now as they were ten thousand years ago. As humans, we cannot claim that reserve in our conduct. We want to create a perfect human being and then clone it. The laws of nature are the rules we should follow.

There is also a lack of concern at the corporate level for the wellbeing of employees. For example, in the BP Deepwater Horizon explosion, eleven people lost their lives. These individuals have value to the company and to their family. It is only just that their family should be compensated for the individual's giving and for their family's loss.

The people here on earth are just too good at going against a myriad of things in nature.

Many churches ask for a tithe, a 10% donation to support the church. Imagine if the world's wealthiest, like the Koch brothers, George Soros, or Carlos Slim were to tithe to their governments. What if they paid their taxes like everyone else, but in addition they tithed from what remains and that money was used to directly benefit the uneducated, the homeless, the veterans, and those dependent on healthcare. What if this money were to go back to the people, rather than to political organizations or any kind of organization with an agenda.

The Bible is full of stories that show that the Almighty is not interested in individuals that are loaded with wealth, if they are not sharing. The whore of Babylon depicted in *Revelations 17* is not sharing.

In his book *The Shaping of America,* Page Smith shows that the intent of the constitution was to have all the resources of the country shared equally. The founding fathers did not intend for there to be extremely rich and or extremely poor. Resources were to be distributed evenly. Some venturesome and hardworking souls would be able to gain a bit more, but not enough to result in the extreme class divisions we have today.

That our society is sick is obvious. Extreme examples are the shooters in the schools. Close behind that are shootings of policemen. But some all too common examples are of a very low nature, like the big man spanking the boy with too much emphasis.

With all this to endure, an earthling is working to improve his soul, his body and mind. Where does he start, and which of the myriad of temptations should he strive to avoid? The reason for the command for men to be fruitful and multiply is that is the only avenue God has for Him to retake the one third of the host that was taken by Satan. God is hopeful that you as a follower will entice your children to get the SPARK. Then we are to be celibate adherents to attain His favor and enter into the kingdom of Heaven.

Get Smarter. This is what God wants all of us to do, get smarter. The only trouble is the manner in which He has the authors write this all down. You will not get the answers from reading the scriptures like an automaton; you must study them.

Is there a caste system, based on the level of learning in one's soul? Some think so. As a part of His cloak, or a thimble full of His wisdom, you have been here since the beginning, part of the Creator. As for the game the Almighty and Satan play with these poor souls here on earth who are striving to learn something, it must be funny and interesting for them to watch us play, using our free will, often with too much freedom.

The Father in heaven should not need to hold a club over your head and the promise of heaven for you to be honest. The truly honest person is honest simply to be honest, honestly. It is very difficult to return the extra cash the teller has given you in error. Some do it, and are finely compensated, as they can sleep at night. Are you one of these??

Putting oneself in the midst of all that is happening here on earth should be avoided as much as possible. That is the first result of the study of metaphysics - it keeps you out of the worldly things and it keeps you thinking. When one is occupied with providing for a family, however, it is necessary to be in the throes of life here on earth. It can be hard to keep your balance.

The pursuit of enlightenment is not for everyone. Many are called, but few are chosen. The meaning is hidden. You are not chosen. It is your job to go after the deep spiritual places. Your soul must take control of the mind in this body, and fol-low the rules from above. The Creator embedded deep in the heart and minds of mortals the love of the flesh. It was necessary for animals to reproduce. The pain in child bearing is considerable. In an effort to keep the animals flourishing, an attraction was paramount. There are many that do not desire this depth of spiritualism. It is my aim to lure you into my trap, with thoughts.

In the *Rubaiyat of Omar Khayyam*, there is a line, "Make Game of that which makes as much of Thee." You should be laughing when playing the learning game.

> *But leave the Wise to wrangle, and with me*
> *The Quarrel of the Universe let be:*
> *And, in some corner of the Hubbub coucht*
> *Make Game of that which makes as much of Thee.*

When and if you get the Spark to engage in the Pursuit of Truth Profound, it will open up a world that you did not know existed. Diligent study will lead the student to deeper insights. My advice is to find some ideology that you are comfortable with and stick to it. There is no real truth that covers it all. The Pursuit is pleasing, and you will better understand the old adage from the Bible, "The peace of mind that surpasses all understanding, will keep your heart and mind in true knowledge of God." This is real relaxing. Try it. You'll like it.

Truth Profound is an effort, a learning task that is never to be completely conquered. Education never ends. My lamp of light in the chandelier of life is not that bright. With that confession, I will share this true story about myself. I was taking banjo lessons from Ray Allotta in Hicksville, Long Island. After my lesson, a young man of nine or ten came in for his lesson. This young man played very well. With Ray's help, he could sing a song he knew and play it on the banjo.

I asked Ray how many lessons it would take for me to play like that. Ray, as honest as a man can be, replied, "There are not enough lessons available. Not in a life time." We have now established the level of my brightness. You're probably saying to yourself, "So Mac, why are you taking on this work??" Because I'm a warrior in this worldly battle with Satan, and I want to share my warrior tactics with you. My strength is from the Bible.

Back to the Soul and the beginning of all things: Were you there? But of course! God asks Job, "Where were you when I laid the foundations of the universe?" *(Job 38:4)* The Bible states that Christ was here in the beginning, and so were you.

Conclusion

The beginning of this ending has taken my thoughts clear away. Love for my enemies, scientists with their penchant for facts, is the basis. We earthlings are not composed of brain matter that can fathom the how, where, and why of this universe, let alone its origin. Where did the material for the universe come from? Science has no more of an answer than the God fearing-populace has with their beliefs. My suggestion is to take some facts and labor over them to a fine degree. Your body is the place to start. Use your brain in the pursuit of these simple facts. We are not all created equally, and you could start by looking for the facts behind that thought. Does evolution throw away the book of rules? That can't be the case, for the rules of nature are immutable.

Homo sapiens, humans, are a contrary bunch. They think they don't have to follow the rules of nature. They make up their own rules as they travel along the road of life here on earth and hope they are doing right.

Hope is the key word in my extensive closing statement. When you buy some stock, you *hope* that it goes favorably for you. When you drive your car you *hope* that there is not an accident or a breakdown. When you marry, you *hope* for the best. Hope is heavier than gravity. I *hope* that this next remark is correct.

The passage "in all thy getting, get thee wisdom and understanding" is not just a Bible thumper's remark. In the *Rubaiyat*, Omar the tentmaker, said "leave the wise to be. Come with ol' Khayyam and take the daughter of the vine to spouse." It is blatantly obvious to me that you are challenged to learn from day one.

The Bible thumpers all believe that death's door is a joyous spot, but as Omar remarked, just don't arrive there with an empty glass.

The final quatrain of the Omar Khayyam's Rubaiyat:

> *And when like her, oh Saki, you shall pass*
> *Among the Guests Star-scatter'd on the Grass,*
> *And in your joyous errand reach the spot*
> *Where I made One—turn down an empty Glass!*

This ol' dummy has a fireside chat with the Almighty from time to time, telling him that He may be taking the role as Father a wee bit to far, as He is acting a lot like the fathers we end up with here on earth. For example, your father probably told you at some time that you would learn to make better decisions after you had made a couple of mistakes. Or your earthly father may have suggested you find a hero to model your life after.

When I chide The Almighty on these several instances, what does He say in response? Nothing. He only laughs, just like my earthly father. In *Luke 8:43*, the Father of Jesus, took it upon Himself to heal the lady and did not even hint to His Son that this woman would be healed. What does this mean? God does not need Jesus for anything. The Almighty has put Jesus here for you, me, us.

The purpose of all this malarkey is just to open up a window for some who are willing to go into the deeper passages and look at some of the ancient stories, ideas that have been going around for a long time. Longer than the churches will admit.

If you study hard, the results are amazing; you will end up in a frame of mind that keeps you from judging other people and keeps you from making mistakes that can be avoided. You live in this protective little cocoon that frees you from getting into all the hype and phony splendor of the physical world we live in. You can choose how you cope and how you handle daily life. It is a much lighter load to carry.

Welcome to The Training Ground!

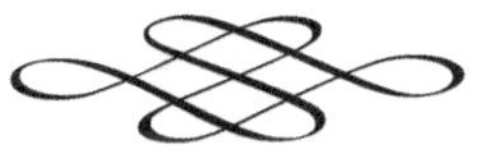

Appendix

Bibliography and Sources

This student has relied on the Bible as the base of rock and concrete while studying other authors' views. My sources have included St. Augustine's *City of God,* Aristotle's treatise *On the Soul,* Dan Brown's *The Da Vinci Code,* as well as his *Inferno,* plus the writings of St. Thomas Aquinas. Jeremy Archer's *Kane and Abel* comes off as an enlightening take on the story of the twin brothers. Of particular interest to me are the Great Seal of the United States, the layout of the streets in Washington DC, the monuments, and the locations.

The biblical quotations were taken from BibleGateway.com and are from the King James version because it is copyright free.

Sidebar information credited to Wikipedia is from en.wikipedia.org.

Recommended Reading

Alexander, Eben. *Proof of Heaven: A Neurosurgeon's Journey into the Afterlife.* Simon & Schuster. 2012. Paperback. Alexander is an American neurosurgeon.

Cahn, Jonathan. *The Harbinger.* Frontline Publishing Inc. 2012. Paperback. An enlightening and very interesting appraisal of the times.

Hesse, Herman. *The Glass Bead Game.* Picador. 2002. Paperback. Also published under the title *Magister Ludi.*

Horn, Thomas. *Zenith 2016.* Defender. 2013. Paperback.

Moody, Raymond. *Coming Back.* Bantam. 1991. Hardcover.

Newton, Michael. *The Journey Of Souls.* Llewellyn Publications. 1994. Paperback. Newton is a hypnotherapist. Though not necessarily into the supernatural, his work in hypnosis has been an eye opener for him. In a hypnotic trance, his clients express memory from deep within the recesses of their minds. The book depicts the journeys the soul must travel in order to raise the level of understanding.
Similar to the accounts in Dr. Raymond A. Moody's book *Coming Back,* several of those with whom Dr. Newton has worked have very similar stories. That these experiences are so similarly expressed by patients compels both of these

authors to admit the possibility of their being true. I here and now will accept this, for my guiding light, in my pursuit of Truth Profound.

After you have read the good Doctors' books, you will have an excellent base for understanding the Almighty's plans for raising your level of empirical wisdom.

Percival, Harold W. *Thinking and Destiny.* The Word Foundation. 1946. Paperback.

Pinch, Geraldine. *A Guide to the Gods, Goddesses, and Traditions of Ancient Egypt.* Oxford University Press. 2004. Paperback. Egyptian Mythology.

Semler, Tracy Chutorian, *All About Eve.* Harper Collins. 1995. Paperback.
Pages 32, 33, 132, and 133 are very important as they describe the nature of the hymen. It is not blocking the discharge of the vagina as people think. There is room for liquid to filter out. This is very important to the understanding of the immaculate conception. It was not so immaculate.

Strong, James. *The New Strong's Expanded Exhaustive Concordance of the Bible.* Thomas Nelson. 2010. Hardcover.

Wilcock, David. *The Source Field Investigations.* Plume. 2012. Paperback.

The papers of Pim Van Lommel, a cardiologist specializing in near-death studies.
Near-death experience in survivors of cardiac arrest: a prospective study in the Netherlands. Lancet 358: 2039-2045. With van Wees, R., Meyers, V. and Elfferich, I. (2001)
About the continuity of our consciousness. Advances in Experimental Medicine and Biology 550: 115-132. (2004)
Near-Death Experience, Consciousness and the Brain. A new concept about the continuity of our consciousness based on recent scientific research on near-death experience in survivors of cardiac arrest. World Futures, The Journal of General Evolution 62: 134-152. (2006)
Consciousness Beyond Life: The Science of the Near-Death Experience (2010, 2011)
Near-death experiences: the experience of the self as real and not as an illusion. Annals of the New York Academy of Sciences 1234: 19-28. (2011)
Nonlocal Consciousness. A concept based on scientific research on near-death experiences during cardiac arrest. Journal of Consciousness Studies 20: 7-48. (2013)

Dear Reader:

Hopefully we have piqued your interest to gain a little knowledge in Archaeology, Astronomy and Science. Their gems of discovery every day, are as beautiful as the full moon eclipse in perigee. These gems will demonstrate that man and nature are and can be in battle all the time. Ole Mother Nature is the winner, so get in line. The subduction here on earth is similar to the black holes in space. The wonder of it all is the repletion of similar happenings from place to place, everywhere, including literature. Where does one concentrate the search for learning? In all the searching you do, it should come back to self as the most important aspect of all your learning. Strive to do a good job of the search and application for reason for the learning.

Have a good day. So long Partner.

Bill McMorrine